Breaking the Silence
A Workbook for Adult Children of Alcoholics

Kathryn Tessmer
Kris Caldwell, Illustrations

D1496916

Breaking the Silence
A Workbook for Adult Children of Alcoholics

A.C.A.T. PRESS
1275 4th Street
Santa Rosa, CA 95404

Copyright© 1986 by Kathryn Tessmer.
Cat Family Illustrations by Kris Caldwell
Adapted by Tamara Slayton
Book and cover design by Tamara Slayton

ISBN 0-9616025-0-3

This book may be directly ordered from A.C.A.T. Press, 1275 4th
Street, Santa Rosa, California, 95404.

First Printing March 1986

Printed in the United States of America

ADULT CHILDREN OF ALCOHOLICS
Meditation Tapes

A Soothing Meditation for the Child-Within

Kathryn Tessmer
Tina Dungan

"The BREAKING THE SILENCE meditation tape gives me comfort in a way I can accept. The images, the music and the message has helped me to find relief from the inside out."

Mike, age 27

...

"Wonderful words, wonderful voice, exquisite music! This tape offers gentle guidance to parts of me I sometimes neglect. WELCOME HOME is a great meditation tape."

Erica, age 35

A Loving Meditation for the Weary Soul

Kathryn Tessmer
Tina Dungan

BREAKING THE SILENCE:
*A Soothing Meditation for the Child-Within
by Kathryn Tessmer and Tina Dungan
45 Min. Cassette, $7.95*

WELCOME HOME:
*A Loving Meditation for the Weary Soul
by Kathryn Tessmer and Tina Dungan
45 Min. Cassette, $7.95*

A.C.A.T. Press

Special products for a special problem

SHIP ORDER TO:

Name _____

Address _____

City _____ State ____ Zip _____

DISCOUNT SCHEDULE			
Book	**1-5** $11.95	**6-15** $10.95	**16 & Over** $8.95
Tape	$7.95	$6.95	$4.95

PRODUCTS	QUANTITY	DISCOUNT	TOTAL
Breaking the Silence Workbook			
Breaking the Silence Tape			
Welcome Home Tape			

Tax Info. add 6% for California Residents

Postage and Handling
 *Add $2.00 for purchase under $20
 *Add 10% of total purchase from $20 to $50
 *Add 6% of total purchase for over $50

Send order to:
A.C.A.T. Press
1275 4th Street
Santa Rosa, CA
95404
707 526-4370

Sub Total	
Tax	
Postage & Handling	
Grand TOTAL	

Breaking the Silence

A WORKBOOK FOR ADULT CHILDREN OF ALCOHOLICS

KATHRYN TESSMER

TABLE OF CONTENTS

ACKNOWLEDGMENTS

For several years, I worked as a Social Worker in residential treatment facilities for "emotionally disturbed" adolescent boys. Indeed their behavior often disturbed me. However, I became aware of a common link between the boys and their family systems that helped me to explain their disturbing behavior. The link was alcoholism! Since the boys were the "identified patients" it was difficult for them and their families to see their current problems as stemming from their alcoholic family. As a staff we began to focus our treatment on the "real problem"; alcoholism and its effects on the family.

Since the boys followed the basic rules: don't talk, don't trust, don't feel; providing treatment that reached them was difficult. Attempts at simply treating the dysfunctional behaviors were met with incredible opposition and little to no results.

Realizing that a new treatment approach was necessary brought me to the door of my friend, Kris Caldwell, a graphic artist. I asked Kris to draw pictures of family dynamics that would stimulate memories and feelings of growing up in an alcoholic family. I shared with her some of the stories and experiences of Children of Alcoholics. We decided to use cats rather than people to express alcoholic family dynamics. Through the use of the written exercises and the Cat Family pictures, the boys broke their silent bond and talked about their alcoholic families. NO LONGER WERE THEY TO BLAME! Through the recognition of the effects of alcoholism came relief for the whole family. In fact, group therapy became a welcomed rather than a forced activity for the boys and their families.

Since the "back door" method of writing and story-telling proved to be effective with adolescents, I re-wrote the workbook for adults.

To the boys, their families and staff and the many Adult Children of Alcoholics who have contributed to the *Breaking the Silence* workbook, I AM GRATEFUL! Your stories and inspiration have made writing and publishing this workbook possible for me.

WITH SPECIAL APPRECIATION FOR THE FOLLOWING PEOPLE:

KRIS CALDWELL, Illustrator and Graphic Artist
For the creation of the Cat Family pictures and for your sensitivity and understanding of the feelings and experiences of Children of Alcoholics, **THANK YOU!**

TAMARA SLAYTON, Graphic Artist, Book Design and Production Manager
For your talent as a graphic artist and design specialist and for your management and guidance of the book production—you've made this incredible project a smooth passage for me, **THANK YOU!**

CLAUDIA NORBY, Editor
For your excellent feedback and ideas and for your caring and support—this has meant so much, **THANK YOU!**

LORI BUCKLEY, Typist
For your steady work at the word processor and your kindness and support, **THANK YOU!**

MARY HARRINGTON, Editor
For your excellent editing and your sensitive criticisms, **THANK YOU!**

IN ACKNOWLEDGMENT OF:

CLAUDIA BLACK, author of *IT WILL NEVER HAPPEN TO ME*
SHARON WEGSCHEIDER-CRUSE, author of *ANOTHER CHANCE, Hope and Health for the Alcoholic Family*
Your leadership in the area of Adult Children of Alcoholics and Co-dependency has strongly influenced my personal recovery as well as my professional growth. *IT WILL NEVER HAPPEN TO ME* and *ANOTHER CHANCE, Hope and Health for the Alcoholic Family* are both so clear and compassionate it seemed unnecessary to write about what's already been written so well. *BREAKING THE SILENCE, A Workbook for Adult Children of Alcoholics* is intended to be used in conjunction with these two outstanding books.

CHAPTER ONE

STAGES OF RECOVERY

As a nation of Children of Alcoholics stands up and identifies with the movement of Adult Children of Alcoholics, a tremendous breakthrough of denial is taking place. It is estimated that between 25 and 28 million people in this country have an alcoholic parent. Many Adult Children of Alcoholics either become alcoholic themselves, or marry an alcoholic, or both, continuing the cycle of the family disease of alcoholism. Most of these children are faced with common problems in adulthood, which often go unrecognized as stemming from their alcoholic families.

Adult Children of Alcoholics frequently experience chronic feelings of anxiety, depression and stress due to the emotional and environmental conditions of the alcoholic home. The chaotic, inconsistent, and sometimes, sadistic behavior of the alcoholic or co-dependent parent has left its mark on generation after generation. When alcohol is identified as the central problem in our families, from which other problems stem, it becomes possible to understand the disease of alcoholism and to grow beyond the limitations of mere survival.

Children of Alcoholics are claiming their identity and power through the recognition of the effects of alcoholism on the family. ***"I AM AN ADULT CHILD OF AN ALCOHO-LIC,"*** is an empowering statement. It recognizes the adult, as well as the child-within who may still feel confused, afraid and alone. It is our way of claiming our history and breaking the denial. It is the beginning of recovery.

The Stages of Recovery closely resemble those of the grief process. Our healing as Adult Children of Alcoholics is in the recognition of our childhood losses and the re-emergence of the natural grieving process. The Stages of Recovery are:

MEMORY AND FEELING RESTIMULATION AND RESOLUTION

TURNING PAIN, SHAME AND BLAME INTO FOCUSED ANGER

BACKSTEPPING FOR MORE RESOLUTION

RE-EMERGENCE OF GRIEF AND JOY

LIVING IN THE HERE AND NOW

Memory and Feeling Restimulation and Resolution

The denial or loss of memories of significant events or periods in our lives is a common problem for Children of Alcoholics. Some of us feel relieved since what we do remember is so unpleasant, who would want to remember more? However, for many others, it is a greater relief to understand and remember what it was like for us as children so that we can begin to make real choices rather than continue to react as if we were still children in an alcoholic home.

Most of us need memory restimulation from the stories and experiences of other Children of Alcoholics in order to remember our childhoods. It is not uncommon for some Children of Alcoholics to have little or no memories prior to seven or eight years old. On the other end of the spectrum are those of us who remember our childhoods in vivid color and detail. The memories are intact but the feelings are well hidden under the lid called "numb." Some of us have other "lid" feelings that act as our primary vehicle for expression of feelings such as anger, hurt or guilt.

There are many feelings that people have access to. In fact, not only are there many feelings, but they come in ranges of intensity (e.g., furious - angry - irritated). It is important for Children of Alcoholics to identify accurately feelings in the moment so that they can be dealt with more appropriately. Accurately identifying feelings reduces stress and helps us to be in the moment rather than reacting to current life situations from the past. The restimulation of feelings and memories is an essential step in recovery. For us to get well, support groups seem to be expedient and positive. **WE GOT SICK IN A FAMILY; WE CAN GET WELL IN A GROUP.**

Most of us remember our experiences from a child's point of view. Even though you may have "acted" like an adult as a child, your intellectual abilities and judgments were limited. They were not limited for a child expected to deal with responsibilities that were age-appropriate. However, they were limited in terms of handling adult responsibilities and decisions. Memory distortions are often realized and resolved during memory and feeling restimulation.

Our healing begins as we understand our predicament as children so that we can forgive ourselves and others as adults. An example of memory and feeling restimulation and resolution is given by Linda. She is a forty-five year old nurse, mother, spouse and oldest child in a large family. Linda is an Adult Child of an Alcoholic.

"I was very close to my grandmother as a young child. In fact, Grandma was the most loving and accepting adult in my life. When I was ten years old, my Grandma died. I was told that she died in a coma. Nothing more was said, and I had a feeling that it was not a subject to bring up again. Grandma's death went into the bag of unmentionables—the Silence. I felt the loss of my grandmother deeply. She was the only person that I could really be a child with. I was the oldest of six and was very responsible for the needs of my siblings and my parents. I couldn't understand why Grandma's life and death fell into the Silence—I only knew that the "Don't Talk Rule" was intact and to survive I followed it.

"I felt denied of my grief for Grandma by my parents and the Silence. I couldn't understand why Grandma would leave me. I loved her so much, and I knew she loved me, too. I felt responsible for Grandma's leaving me. I came to believe that if I love someone deeply, they'll leave me. Put simply, I can't have what I want. Of course, I went through life proving this over and over again.

"As an adult, I participated in a Breaking the Silence Workshop. I knew my parents' drinking was more than social, and that it had affected my life. In discussing my family and childhood experiences, I came to realize that my grandma was also an alcoholic. I had forgotten the arguments that my parents had about her and her drinking. Through my adult intellect and my childhood memories, I was able to understand the real reason why Grandma left me.

"My grandma died in an alcohol and drug induced coma—possibly a suicide. No wonder the "Don't Talk Rule" was dropped like a dark shroud over Grandma. Back then, suicide in a Catholic family not only brought shame to the family, but the suicidal victim was forever doomed to Purgatory.

"I felt a tremendous relief and comfort in being able to piece together the truth about Grandma. It enabled me to be angry. I am angry at the disease of alcoholism that took my grandma away from me."

For Linda, as for so many Adult Children of Alcoholics, memory resolution is very healing and allows for the continuous progression through the grief cycle. Not only was Linda able to grieve for Grandma with support from the group, she was also able to see that she was no longer unworthy and incapable of sustaining love and intimacy in her life. She was no longer a victim of the script, "I can't have what I want," and began to experience a receptivity to love that she had never allowed herself before.

Turning Shame, Blame and Pain Into Focused Anger

For many Children of Alcoholics, shame, blame and pain are the primary extinguishers of focused anger. A vague, but omnipresent, feeling of hopelessness seems to weigh us down. Turning shame, blame and pain into focused anger requires a willingness to connect current and past feelings with childhood memories. As we connect our feelings of shame, blame and pain to growing up in an alcoholic environment, we naturally begin to feel the anger that has been waiting to surface for so long. As we remember and resolve our feelings we find that we can then focus our anger on the real culprit in the alcoholic family: *THE DISEASE OF ALCOHOLISM.*

The path of recovery is not one of hatred but of love. We must make an honest inventory of the effects of the disease of alcoholism on the family. This requires that we look closely at the behavior, attitudes and feelings of our parents, siblings and ourselves. Only in this way can we get beyond our resentments that hold our love and our compassions for our parents at bay. It is a given that we love our parents. Being angry at them during early recovery allows for more opportunity to accept and love them in the way we've always hoped for—unconditionally.

Some Children of Alcoholics need a period of abstinence from contact with their parents and siblings so that they can feel the anger. A brief period of abstinence from our families can allow us to establish stronger emotional and physical boundaries. These boundaries help us to avoid developing new resentments as we clear out the old.

Allowing ourselves to feel anger requires safety. For the most part, our anger is not a danger to anyone but ourselves. However, to allow ourselves the opportunity to focus anger and express it, we need a lot of support. For many Children of Alcoholics, support groups that are structured and well-guided by a group leader provide an environment which allows for the safe expression of anger. Discharging old anger can be very frightening for us.

As we uncover our childhood losses, we uncover the old anger. In the beginning, it may seem overwhelming. The first few layers of fury may be greater than you thought possible.

As with most feelings that have been stuffed, denied or buried, the initial re-experiencing of that feeling will be out of proportion to reality. In time and in recovery, removing the lid of anger will be easier and easier, and the results will be positive and rewarding.

We can break the cycle of self destructiveness by expressing anger safely and constructively. We cannot do this alone. With the support of other Children of Alcoholics we can step through the fires of anger to the other side—compassion, forgiveness and love.

Backstepping for More Resolution

Many Children of Alcoholics have an overwhelming urge to be unique. This urge will overshadow a desire for belonging to and identification with Adult Children of Alcoholics as a group. This urgency for uniqueness may be played out in several ways. The most common way we resist recovery is through "comparative misery." Children of Alcoholics will find anyone whose story and life are more miserable or problematic than their own to reinstate the denial. It often sounds like this: *"My childhood wasn't so bad. I mean it certainly wasn't as bad as everyone else's here. I don't really feel as miserable as all of you. I really feel sorry for you."*

It is true that wherever you go in life you will find someone else worse off, especially if you're seeking a way out. For most of us, denial has a way of creeping back into our consciousness, especially when we're fearful of our ability to cope with reality or our feelings. Backstepping for More Resolutions is often a necessary step in order to reach a deeper level of self-understanding and resolution.

Recovery is not a linear experience. It is not a sequence of steps and actions resulting in perfection. Recovery is a circular experience leading to an unveiling of our true selves on deeper levels. It is a way of life that relieves us of the notion that if we do the "right things," we will become the "right person." We already are the "right person;" we need only risk more awareness and sensitivity to our feelings. Therefore, Backstepping for More Resolution is a part of the process that rejoins us with ourselves.

At this stage in recovery, many Children of Alcoholics express ambivalence towards working on recovery. Previous behaviors and thoughts become appealing. These previous behaviors and thoughts are typically our survival strategies which are familiar and easy. Again, we often seek the easy way out. Getting well does take effort, and being human (rather than mechanical) does cause pain. **"NO PAIN; NO GAIN,"** truly applies to this stage of recovery.

Fortunately, at this stage in recovery, it will be difficult to turn back the clock and remove the insights and the hope. For the alcoholic who has known sobriety and its benefits, and then has a slip and drinks again, drinking will never be the same. Similarly, Children of Alcoholics find that the old ways of surviving just aren't as satisfying now that we know a better way to live. The glimmer of hope that we've always dreamed of is now visible and possible for us, and we can no longer deny ourselves the love and joy that are our human right.

Re-emergence of Grief and Joy

For much of our childhood and adolescence as Children of Alcoholics, our feelings of grief over minor and major losses in our lives were denied or minimized. It was not acceptable to express our real feelings. Many of us learned to camouflage them so well that even we were not aware of the sadness and pain of growing up in an alcoholic home. Often by utilizing our survival roles, we found other ways to channel our pain rather than acknowledge it or feel it. This was not a choice; it was a necessity.

Because there was little or no time to resolve feelings of loss and pain, many of us have developed a delayed awareness of feelings. It is not uncommon for Children of Acoholics to realize that they are angry or hurt about a specific incident or conversation two or three days, or sometimes weeks, later. This delayed awareness of feelings often creates stress and discomfort, which lasts longer since it is denied. For some, delayed awareness in the moment creates feelings of being "crazy" since what may be happening in the moment (e.g., a positive interaction with a friend) may be overshadowed by an uneasiness (e.g., anxiety, fear, anger) that doesn't relate to the present situation.

Other Children of Alcoholics have been known to delay grief of a major loss, such as a spouse, child or parent, for years. Delayed grief is often more painful and debilitating, especially when the denial finally lifts, and awareness of the loss sets in.

As we begin to recover as Children of Alcoholics, there is a re-emergence of grief. As a mother who loses her beloved child to death grieves over her loss, so do we as Children of Alcoholics grieve over our countless losses, especially the loss of our childhood. We allow the pain, memories and sadness to re-emerge. In support groups, we find a family of friends who share in our grief. We can heal our wounds, regrets and lost opportunities in a safe and constructive way.

Many Children of Alcoholics find the re-emergence of grief is more tolerable than the depression and anxiety that we know so well. In the past, fear and uncertainty stood in the way of acknowledging our loss, as well as our family's losses. Although we cannot change history, we can change ourselves today. We can begin to make new choices and realize our new-found opportunities for living. We no longer need to blame others, especially our parents, for our current problems. We begin to heal together.

We also experience a re-emergence of joy. Many Children of Alcoholics have not only repressed sad and painful memories from their childhood, but also pleasant and happy ones. These memories are a positive payoff in the process of recovery. They also fill in the picture of our childhood with a brush of realism that we have denied. Most Children of Alcoholics have had joyful, loving moments with their parents and siblings. The re-emergence of these memories opens the door to the joy that we are so capable of giving and receiving. These positive memories remind us that the real enemy is not our parents but the disease of alcoholism.

Living in the Here and Now

Many Adult Children of Alcoholics have made a tremendous effort to make up for the lack of guidance and support in their childhood through self-help books, seminars and counseling. Often the results are positive, at least for a while. And then we're back to zero again, in terms of dealing with our self-destructive tendencies and feelings of self-hatred and inadequacy. Many of us have been seduced into a false hope of being fixed. Similarly, many alcoholics go into treatment for financial problems, marital problems, sexual problems, etc. and do not deal with the "real problem" which is the drinking and its effects. We, as Children of Alcoholics, have also sought treatment in the same way, hoping to fix the behaviors and ignore our feelings and the past. Finally, after years of frustration, followed by hopelessness, we are now dealing with the "real problem"—growing up in an alcoholic home.

As we accept our history and put it into its proper perspective, we can begin to learn the basic living skills that are so easy and natural to learn. By learning to live in the here and now, we begin to strengthen and encourage new values and beliefs about ourselves. We value our right to be. Simply, to be alive.

Healing old wounds and learning new behaviors takes time. There's no need to hurry! Each new discovery is a gift. Allowing ourselves to receive this renewed gift of life is its own reward, one moment at a time. Recovery also requires a willingness to experience our human emotions and accept our

human frailties. In this way we no longer need to numb out reality. We can live in the here and now and today it is our choice.

In recovery we develop a new identity, which allows us to integrate new beliefs and feelings through behavior change. An old belief that maintains compartmentalized behavior is, *"I can't do something I've never done before. I can't go somewhere that I haven't been before. I can't learn things that I haven't learned before. I must stay safe in my niche of survival."* In recovery we form new beliefs which allow for expansion and enhancement in areas of little or no expertise. An example of this is: *"I'm trying out new things, going new places, learning new ways of being. I'm breaking out of my comfortable niche of survival. I'm not doing this alone but with the support of other Children of Alcoholics who understand and help me."*

Another example of a belief that maintains compartmentalized feelings is: *"I am angry all the time. If only everyone else would change, I wouldn't feel angry. YOU make me feel angry."* In recovery we take responsibility for our own feelings. We also develop a greater range of feelings. Therefore, we learn to define our feelings accurately, which reduces stress and helps to guide our expression of feelings. An example of labeling feelings more accurately is: *"I feel angry. No, actually, I feel irritated. Yes, that's more accurate."* We can check our feelings out with other Children of Alcoholics who can help us to know.

Many Children of Alcoholics find that the Al-Anon Recovery Program is a safe and supportive environment for learning basic living skills. Al-Anon is a support group for families and friends of alcoholics.

NO LONGER ARE WE ALONE; WE ARE ALL TOGETHER NOW IN STRENGTH, IN LOVE AND IN RECOVERY!

CHAPTER TWO

HOW TO USE THE WORKBOOK

Breaking the Silence, A Workbook for Adult Children of Alcoholics is designed to stimulate your feelings, memories and pain from growing up in an alcoholic family. It is also a way to assist you in looking at the past in a constructive and supportive way. Finally, after years of silence, comes validation for your experiences, losses and pain. This validation may not come from your parents or siblings. However, it is there when you are willing to break the silence and reach across the barriers of loss and loneliness to recovery. Our stories may be different, but our feelings and grief are often the same. Each child in an alcoholic family carries his or her own personal tragedy. This personal tragedy evolves into generational tragedies, when the cycle of alcoholism and its effects are unbroken. Through the process of recovery—relearning to feel, to trust and to talk—you will find love and understanding beyond your wildest dreams.

Remember the Child

As we share our stories and losses, we come to embrace and remember the child that once was so tender, so small and so fragile. In remembering our small size and our powerlessness, we also learn to recognize the child within each of us that today may be angry, hurt and self-destructive. With love and compassion and a safe environment in which to grow, we enable ourselves to become the loving and happy people that we are meant to be. In recovery, we remember the child as she or he once was, which enables us to truly experience compassion and love for ourselves and for our parents.

In the space provided, paste a photograph of yourself as a child, *or* draw a picture of yourself as a child, *or* select a picture from a magazine that reminds you of yourself as a child. Throughout your writings in the workbook **Remember the Child.** Turn to this page to give yourself perspective on the effects of the disease of alcoholism on such a small and tender being.

With the Support and Listening Ear

As children we learned to keep our feelings, thoughts and desires locked deep down inside. As the family became sicker and sicker with the disease of alcoholism, we became silent. **With the Support and Listening Ear** of a friend, a spouse, a therapist or group you can break out of the isolation and loneliness. There are others just like you who will understand. Recovery of our true selves as loving human beings, free of fear and hatred, is a courageous and powerful act. It is an act of self-love. The silence must be broken and we must say it to another caring person to experience the relief and face the truth of the legacy of alcoholism.

One Chapter at a Time

In recovery, we are patient. In our patience, we learn to accept our losses and our problems with compassion and understanding. To integrate new insights, we need time. We need time to feel the feelings that have long been buried with our childhood memories. As your memories surface, so do the feelings. Taking steps towards recovery may feel like baby steps at first. After a while, it will not be so hard or painful, however, take these steps as naturally and as softly as a child—**One Chapter at a Time.**

Intuit What You Don't Know As Fact

Many Children of Alcoholics feel insecure about their intuition and about their memory recall. "What is real?" "What is normal?" These are common questions of the early recovering child of an alcoholic. For many of us, there was little or no validation for expression of our feelings.

Each member of our family may have kept hidden their real feelings, only manifesting the feelings and thoughts associated with their survival role in the alcoholic family. Oddly enough, we also had an incredible radar system that warned us of impending conflict. Unfortunately, our radar did not necessarily save us or protect us from conflict, criticism or humiliation due to our powerlessness in the situation. The result for many of us is distrust and dismay at our intuition and sensitivity. It didn't save us and often prolonged or extended the fear and anxiety we already knew so well.

In recovery, we can reclaim our intuitions. Unlike during our childhood, today we have choices. We can utilize our intuition to help ourselves and to validate and express our feelings in a safe way. Some of the sections and pictures in the workbook will require you to intuit how other family members felt, thought and reacted to living in an alcoholic family. As best as you can, **Intuit What You Don't Know As Fact.** Generally, we often know how other family members felt, even though much of the communication in our families was guarded, confusing or non-verbal.

Making Alterations

There are several pictures of family dynamics that may help to stimulate your feelings and memories of growing up in an alcoholic family. Some of the pictures may bring an immediate flash of a childhood memory; others may not.

As you work on the Cat pictures and stories, allow yourself to make alterations to fit your family circumstances and dynamics. Some Children of Alcoholics change the sex of the Cats in the pictures, depending upon which parent was alcoholic or co-dependent. Some Children of Alcoholics add to the pictures when it aids in describing a childhood memory or experience. We certainly have an abundance of memories or feelings of things that did or didn't happen because we grew up in an alcoholic family.

Making Alterations may help us to step through our resistance to acknowledging and validating our perceptions and memories that the pictures and stories make available to us. Our resistance to truly seeing our alcoholic family and parents as they are and were is often great. This resistance is normal. However, recovery requires us to remember and to feel the pain.

The Language of Feelings

Each Cat in each picture will have one to three lines next to their cartoon bubble. These lines are for the identification of feelings that you think they had in that situation. Learning **The Language of Feelings** is an important step towards recovering all the feelings we have denied or numbed out over the years. Many Children of Alcoholics only have access to feelings associated with their survival roles. Reclaiming our feelings takes work and practice. It may feel risky to do at first but it will help you to bridge the gap between your true self and the role you play to avoid feelings. For many of us, realizing that we did have feelings in our childhood, even though they were denied, helps us to understand why we react so negatively to feeling our feelings today. Again, what you don't know as absolute fact, intuit. There is no right or wrong answer. Our writings are respectfully subjective, therefore, our intuitions are ours and are acceptable.

Each picture also has a line for the title of the story. These are your stories and you can claim them as your own.

The Spoken from the Unspoken Words

In each picture, there are cartoon bubbles for the dialogue or thoughts of each cat in the picture. For many of us, we walk through life with a tyrannical and martyring parent who verbally abuses us internally. This internal dialogue has had a powerful effect on our self-esteem. For many Children of Alcoholics, the evidence of their childhood misery lies in the awareness of this horrifying inner dialogue of verbal abuse we do to ourselves. "Stupid." "What's wrong with you?" "I'm not worthy of love from him/her." Where did we learn to name-call, berate and reject ourselves?

It may be helpful to distinguish **The Spoken from the Unspoken Words.** For many of us, we learned not to say out loud our feelings or thoughts. We learned to lie, hide or disguise them. It is no wonder that as adults, even in situations when the truth would be better, we continue to lie, hide, or disguise our real feelings and thoughts. To distinguish the spoken from the unspoken words, you may want to use quotation marks on the words said aloud and capitalize without quotation marks words that are unspoken. This may help you to see just how many double messages, as well as verbal abuse, you received or were around as a child.

FEELINGS LIST

LOVE	EXCITED	CARING
HATE	SURPRISED	CAREFREE
ANGER	SHOCKED	FEAR
FRUSTRATION	AFRAID	MEAN
GUILT	IMPORTANT	AGGRESSIVE
ANXIETY	REJECTED	IRRITATED
WORRY	DEPRESSED	JUSTIFIED
HURT	NERVOUS	DEFENSIVE
TIRED	GRIEF	DEPENDENT
CONFUSED	INADEQUATE	ISOLATED
CURIOUS	DISAPPOINTED	ALONE
HOPELESS	LONELY	INDEPENDENT
HOPEFUL	BORED	TRAPPED
APPRECIATIVE	BLAMED	POWERFUL
HELPLESS	SELF-DOUBT	NEEDED
OVERWHELMED	DESERTED	CONFIDENT
PRESSURED	BETRAYED	WANTED
SURE	PEACEFUL	SECURE
UNSURE	ENTHUSIASTIC	INSECURE
SATISFIED	EMPTY	CAUTIOUS
RELIEF	MAD	VULNERABLE
JOY	SYMPATHY	TENDER
SCARED	EMBARRASSED	RAGE
HOSTILITY	SHY	ACCEPTED
CONFUSION	TERROR	NURTURING
AGGRAVATED	ABUSED	WEAK
PROTECTIVE	FLEXIBLE	DECEIVED
POSSESSIVE	MISUNDERSTOOD	SELF-DEFEATING
HAPPY	PROUD	DISGUSTED
SAD	PLEASED	CONTENT

CHAPTER THREE
CAT FAMILY STORIES

EXAMPLE OF CAT FAMILY PICTURE

I HATE YOU.
I HATE YOU.
I HATE YOU.
I CAN'T HEAR A WORD
YOU'RE SAYING.

●NON-VERBAL
COMMUNICATIONS

OVERWHELMED

TRAPPED

ANGRY

"Get in here right now.
Do you call that room
clean? I told you to clean
it. Now do it, or I'll give
you a whippin' you won't
forget."

●VERBAL
COMMUNICATIONS

LONELY

MEAN

POSSESSIVE

●FEELINGS

TITLE
EVERYBODY'S TALKIN' AT ME

The Cat Family Story

TITLE: *One's Too Many, One Thousand's Not Enough*

GIVE THE NAMES AND AGES OF ALL THE CATS INVOLVED IN THE SCENE

Mother – 27
Father – 35

WHERE IS THE SCENE TAKING PLACE?

The living room.

WHAT LED UP TO THIS SCENE?

My father comes home from another bad day at work. He hates his job as a bookkeeper/clerk. He often says that if he hadn't had to get married, he would have gone to college and been a great success. He's in one of his moods. My mother acts like she's walking on egg shells.

TELL WHY THE CATS ARE DOING WHAT THEY ARE DOING.

My mother tries to give him what he wants. She still feels guilty and ashamed that she was pregnant before their marriage even after all these years. She pretends that we are a normal happy family. She also pretends that my father can have a drink with dinner like normal people. She drinks too. My father drinks to express his feelings. He seems to need a drink to say what he wants or how he feels. When he doesn't drink, he's like a bomb just ready to go off. My mother drinks to placate him. He doesn't like to drink alone. Occasionally, they have big fights when they've both had a lot to drink.

WHAT IS THE OUTCOME OF THE STORY?

My father is dissatisfied with everything . . . his job, my mother, me, everything! My father tries to limit his drinking, but he can't stop after one drink. For him, one's too many, and one thousand's not enough. After several drinks, he begins staring at the floor and lamenting, "You'd be better off without me. I'm no good. I can't do anything right . . ." My mother can't face reality. She tries to reason with him when he's in this state of mind. It's disgusting to listen to—I could never understand her. Later, she puts him to bed, and when we get up in the morning, it's never mentioned or discussed.

Fifteen years later, my father committed suicide. He was drunk at the time. I was 25 then. After he died, I picked up where he left off—I became an alcoholic, too.

The Cat Family Story

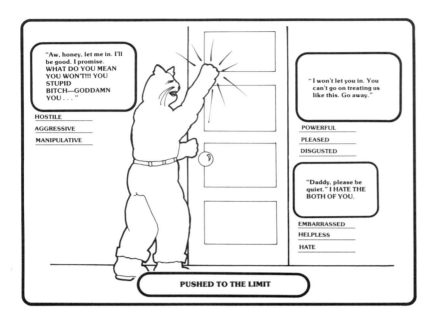

"Aw, honey, let me in. I'll be good. I promise. WHAT DO YOU MEAN YOU WON'T!!! YOU STUPID BITCH—GODDAMN YOU . . ."

HOSTILE
AGGRESSIVE
MANIPULATIVE

" I won't let you in. You can't go on treating us like this. Go away."

POWERFUL
PLEASED
DISGUSTED

"Daddy, please be quiet." I HATE THE BOTH OF YOU.

EMBARRASSED
HELPLESS
HATE

PUSHED TO THE LIMIT

TITLE: *Pushed to the Limit*

GIVE THE NAMES AND AGES OF ALL THE CATS INVOLVED IN THE SCENE

Dad – 38

Mom – 37

Diane – 12

WHERE IS THE SCENE TAKING PLACE?

The front porch.

WHAT LED UP TO THIS SCENE?

My mom and dad are fighting, as usual. I just finished putting the little ones to bed. Dad has been drinking most of the evening. He and Mom begin arguing about the same old thing; his drinking. They are standing in the front hall by the door. Mom is so mad she shoves him out the door.

TELL WHY THE CATS ARE DOING WHAT THEY ARE DOING

Dad's now on the front porch banging on the door. My mom looks very satisfied with herself—she's gotten back at him for some of the misery he's caused her. Of course, Dad wants to get back into the house. Mom won't let him in. She'd like to ignore him, but he's yelling obscenities. I feel angry at both of them. They're acting like two year olds. Mostly, I feel embarrassed because the neighbors are probably able to hear him. Mom wants to scare Dad, so she threatens to call the police. She seems to want to get rid of him. But no, he just gets worse and yells more. She sends me off to call the police. I feel so angry, but I push my feelings away. Someone has to take charge of things.

WHAT IS THE OUTCOME OF THE STORY?

The police come and talk to my dad. Then they talk to my mom. Both of my parents become very polite and respectable while the police are there. It's very strange. After the police leave, my parents argue for a while longer until my dad finally collapses and passes out.

I check on my brothers and sisters, and then I go to bed. Finally, when it's quiet, I pray to God that no one noticed.

The Cat Family Story

POWERFUL

AFRAID

HURT

"You dumb bitch, where's my dinner? Don't tell me to shut up!"

"Shut up! Don't scream at me. Don't hurt me!"

OH NO—
NOT AGAIN!
WHY DOES SHE PUT UP WITH HIM!

SNIF!

HELPLESS

ZZZZ . . .

EMPTY

OH NO, NOT AGAIN!

TITLE: *Oh No, Not Again!*

GIVE THE NAMES AND AGES OF ALL THE CATS INVOLVED IN THE SCENE

Mom – 36   *Brad – 8*
Stepfather – 38   *Suzy – 9*
John – 12

WHERE IS THE SCENE TAKING PLACE?

This is one of the many apartments that my family lived in while I was growing up.

WHAT LED UP TO THIS SCENE?

My stepfather didn't come straight home from work. He stopped off at the local bar and got drunk. He and my mother are not able to pay the rent so he's been on a binge drunk with what's left of the money that my mom borrowed from my aunt. My mother is nervous about getting kicked out of the apartment. (It wouldn't be the first time—or the last.)

TELL WHY THE CATS ARE DOING WHAT THEY'RE ARE DOING

My stepfather comes in and starts a fight about dinner not being ready for him. He usually finds something to fight about so that they don't get to fight about what's really going on—that he's been drinking away all their money. My mother is so low and beaten down she lets him blame her for not making dinner for him. My sister Suzy is crying quietly. She is very sensitive and gets really scared when my parents fight. My brother Brad is either asleep or pretending to be asleep. He seems to be able to disappear when anyone is fighting. I'm (John) wide awake, just in case I need to call the police. I feel frightened, but I don't say anything because if I do he'll just yell at me too. I lie there knowing there isn't anything I can do to stop him.

WHAT IS THE OUTCOME OF THE STORY?

One night my mother decides to leave my stepfather. We're going to get kicked out of the apartment anyway so we pack our things up and run away. My mother meets another man who seems nice at first . . . then after a while he spends more and more time drinking, and it's the same situation all over again.

The Cat Family Story

I HATE YOU.
I HATE YOU.
I HATE YOU.
I CAN'T HEAR A WORD
YOU'RE SAYING.

OVERWHELMED
TRAPPED
ANGRY

"Get in here right now.
Do you call that room
clean? I told you to clean
it. Now do it, or I'll give
you a whippin' you won't
forget."

LONELY
MEAN
POSSESSIVE

EVERYBODY'S TALKIN' AT ME

TITLE: *Everybody's Talking at Me*

GIVE THE NAMES AND AGES OF ALL THE CATS INVOLVED IN THE SCENE

Mother – 33

Patrick – 8

WHERE IS THE SCENE TAKING PLACE?

On the front porch.

WHAT LED UP TO THIS SCENE?

Mom went out last night with her girlfriends. She came home real late. She was drunk. She said she saw my dad at the bar with another woman. She was really mad, even though they've been separated a long time.

TELL WHY THE CATS ARE DOING WHAT THEY'RE DOING

When my mom gets up in the morning, she doesn't remember very much from the night before. She doesn't remember waking me up and crying about my dad and the other woman. She just wakes up mad. I am the only one around for her to be mad at so she takes it out on me. I try to get away but she catches me before I get past the porch. She starts her "Clean up your room and it'd better be perfect" routine. I feel stupid and guilty. I never do it well enough for her. I think she just doesn't want to be alone, so she makes me stay. It doesn't matter, though, because I end up going away anyway—at least on the inside.

WHAT IS THE OUTCOME OF THE STORY?

I go to my room and wait it out. There's no use trying to figure out what she wants. She always finds one more thing wrong. I play music. I know how to escape her and everyone else who bugs me. I don't hear a word they say.

Later on . . . she takes me to a restaurant for dinner. She's now in a good mood. She expects me to be in one, too. I go along . . . I don't feel like I have any choice.

The Cat Family Story

TITLE: *You're Going To Get It Now!*

GIVE THE NAMES AND AGES OF ALL THE CATS INVOLVED IN THE SCENE

Mom – 36
Jenny – 13
Alice – 6

WHERE IS THE SCENE TAKING PLACE?

In my parents' bedroom.

WHAT LED UP TO THIS SCENE?

My mom takes an afternoon nap every day. She usually puts on her negligee, snacks on crackers, pickles and beer, and reads romance magazines. She sends Jenny and me outside so that she can be alone. She says we get on her nerves.

TELL WHY THE CATS ARE DOING WHAT THEY ARE DOING

Jenny and I are fighting. Jenny tries to control me. She tells me to be quiet or else we'll get in trouble. I get scared and mad because she is wrestling too rough for me. I start crying and go to my mom's bedroom to tell her what Jenny did. When I wake up Mom, she becomes angry. She doesn't care about my feelings. She goes to the closet and gets one of my father's leather belts. She tells us, "You're going to get it now." She begins hitting us. She hits Jenny a lot and blames her for not keeping me under control. She hits Jenny until she cries. She doesn't hit me as much or as hard, because I start crying right away. I feel guilty for getting us in trouble. I feel scared that Jenny will hate me.

WHAT IS THE OUTCOME OF THE STORY?

Jenny and I go outside and sit by the railroad tracks. Jenny looks for sassafrass weeds to make iced tea. After a while she talks to me again. I feel relieved that she doesn't hate me anymore.

I learned not to ask for my mom's help when my older brothers and sisters picked on me. Mom only made it worse so I learned to be tough and make it on my own.

The Cat Family Story

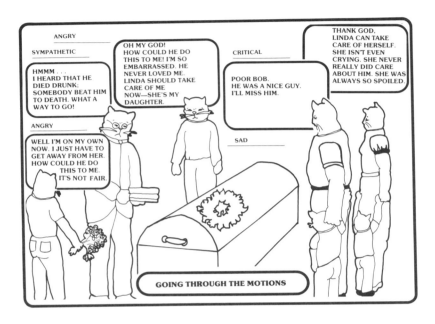

TITLE: *Going Through the Motions*

GIVE THE NAMES AND AGES OF ALL THE CATS INVOLVED IN THE SCENE

Linda – 21   Jack – 28

Mary – 50   Joan – 26

WHERE IS THE SCENE TAKING PLACE?

Funeral Home in Los Angeles.

WHAT LED UP TO THIS SCENE?

The entire family knew my father was in the hospital in critical condition. No one called to tell me—not even my mother. She called me after he died. My father was beaten to death—he was drunk at the time. They never found out who did it or why.

TELL WHY THE CATS ARE DOING WHAT THEY ARE DOING

I (Linda) feel so angry and betrayed that I can't even look at my mother. I'm turned away, isolated from the rest of the family. I'm so angry that I can't cry. My mother seems angry too. I can tell that she is mad at me for not comforting her. I feel pressure from the family to take care of her. I hate it, and I can't do it anymore. So I shut my feelings off and go through the motions of the funeral.

My cousin Joan is very supportive of my mother. She is critical of me and looks at me with disdain. Her husband, Jack, is sad and shows it. He liked my father. He's probably the only one who did.

WHAT IS THE OUTCOME OF THE STORY?

As soon as the funeral was over, I went back to San Francisco as fast as I could. When I was alone in my apartment, I fell apart and cried for sixteen hours. I felt so alone. On Monday I went back to work and acted as if nothing had happened. I was ashamed to tell anyone about my father's death—I didn't want anyone to know how he died. Years later, after I got married, I told my husband. I still felt ashamed, but I felt better for having told someone.

The Cat Family Story

TITLE: *The Last Stop Tavern*

GIVE THE NAMES AND AGES OF ALL THE CATS INVOLVED IN THE SCENE

Mom – 32
Joel – 13
Denise – 7

WHERE IS THE SCENE TAKING PLACE?

At the tavern downtown.

WHAT LED UP TO THIS SCENE?

Mom took Joel and me shopping for school clothes. It was great buying brand new dresses and shoes. Mom wanted a treat too, so she stopped in at the tavern for just one drink. She gave Joel and me fifty cents each for an ice cream cone and says she'll be out in a little while.

TELL WHY THE CATS ARE DOING WHAT THEY ARE DOING

Joel and I are finished with our ice cream cones. We're waiting in front of the tavern for Mom to finish her drink. Mom is having a good time. She looks out the door and sees us and suddenly looks angry. I know we didn't do anything, but it feels like we did because she keeps drinking.

Joel takes over when my mom drinks. He says she'll be awhile, and he is usually right. I feel scared at first, then I feel safe, because I know Joel will take care of us. We go to the car and wait there for my mom.

WHAT IS THE OUTCOME OF THE STORY?

Joel and I fall asleep in the car while we are waiting for Mom. It's dark when she returns to the car. She scares us because she can't get the door open and she is cursing under her breath. Joel gets out of the car and takes the keys. He helps her into the front seat. Joel is 13 years old, but he drives us home anyway. I'm glad, because he's a good driver.

The Cat Family Story

TITLE: *Mr. Big Shot*

GIVE THE NAMES AND AGES OF ALL THE CATS INVOLVED IN THE SCENE

Father – 37
Mother – 34
Elizabeth – 15

Jack – 14
Lisa – 2

WHERE IS THE SCENE TAKING PLACE?

In the kitchen of our house.

WHAT LED UP TO THIS SCENE?

This was nearly a daily ritual. My father focused his anger on my brother Jack. If Jack didn't mouth off, we'd often have a peaceful meal. My father seemed to like to make Jack knuckle under in front of us. If he did mouth off, he'd be slapped around and then sent to his room.

TELL WHY EACH OF THE CATS ARE DOING WHAT THEY ARE DOING

My father is calling Jack names to get him mad. He seemed to get a lot of pleasure out of humiliating him. My mother tended to ignore my father's abuse of Jack. I usually tried to distract or manipulate my father into leaving Jack alone. I felt guilty because my father treated me so differently. I was his little princess. Jack would put up with my father's remarks up to a point. As he got older, he tolerated it less and less which meant he rarely ate dinner with us.

The baby would cry during the fighting and spill her food. She was scared by the loud noises.

WHAT IS THE OUTCOME OF THE STORY?

My father and Jack never got along. By the time he was in his teens, he was using street drugs. By the time he was 16, he was a drug addict. He ended up in a lot of trouble with the law and spent time in jail. I always felt like I never did enough to help him. Sometimes I still feel guilty because he had such a hard life. Today, he's in Alcoholics Anonymous and Narcotics Anonymous, and he's finally getting his life together.

FEELINGS LIST

LOVE	EXCITED	CARING
HATE	SURPRISED	CAREFREE
ANGER	SHOCKED	FEAR
FRUSTRATION	AFRAID	MEAN
GUILT	IMPORTANT	AGGRESSIVE
ANXIETY	REJECTED	IRRITATED
WORRY	DEPRESSED	JUSTIFIED
HURT	NERVOUS	DEFENSIVE
TIRED	GRIEF	DEPENDENT
CONFUSED	INADEQUATE	ISOLATED
CURIOUS	DISAPPOINTED	ALONE
HOPELESS	LONELY	INDEPENDENT
HOPEFUL	BORED	TRAPPED
APPRECIATIVE	BLAMED	POWERFUL
HELPLESS	SELF-DOUBT	NEEDED
OVERWHELMED	DESERTED	CONFIDENT
PRESSURED	BETRAYED	WANTED
SURE	PEACEFUL	SECURE
UNSURE	ENTHUSIASTIC	INSECURE
SATISFIED	EMPTY	CAUTIOUS
RELIEF	MAD	VULNERABLE
JOY	SYMPATHY	TENDER
SCARED	EMBARRASSED	RAGE
HOSTILITY	SHY	ACCEPTED
CONFUSION	TERROR	NURTURING
AGGRAVATED	ABUSED	WEAK
PROTECTIVE	FLEXIBLE	DECEIVED
POSSESSIVE	MISUNDERSTOOD	SELF-DEFEATING
HAPPY	PROUD	DISGUSTED
SAD	PLEASED	CONTENT

CHAPTER FOUR
FEELINGS

Many Children of Alcoholics have difficulty identifying feelings in the moment; we often have delayed feelings. Some of us feel numb or have an absence of feelings. Unexpressed or delayed feelings may build up over time and lead to feeling overwhelmed or out of control.

Generally, most Children of Alcoholics feel the feelings associated with their role in the alcoholic family.

The **Hero or Responsible Child** may feel inadequacy and guilt.

"No matter what I do, it's never good enough."

The **Scapegoat or Acting Out Child** may feel hurt and anger.

"Nobody understands me. I hate them all."

The **Lost or Adjuster Child** may feel shy and lonely.

"I'd just like to be left alone."

The **Mascot or Placator Child** may feel fear and anxiety.

"What if nobody likes me? What if . . . ?"

In alcoholic families, feelings are expressed in extremes, "I love you/I hate you." "You're good/you're bad." "I'm staying/I'm leaving." Children of Alcoholics often react to everyday situations as if life were an ongoing crisis; the rollercoaster effect. This limits our ability to identify feelings; as well as see options that may be available. Self-esteem is built on positive and successful decision making. Impulsive or reactive decision-making does not aid in the development of self-esteem or emotional growth.

IDENTIFYING YOUR PARENTS' EXPRESSION OF FEELINGS MAY HELP YOU TO UNDERSTAND YOUR ABILITY OR LIMITATION IN TERMS OF IDENTIFYING OR EXPRESSING FEELINGS.

PART ONE
Expression of Feelings

From the scale below, select the number that best describes the frequency of emotional expression of your mother, father and yourself.

1 - Never expressed feeling
2 - Rarely expressed feeling
3 - Sometimes expressed feeling
4 - Often expressed feeling
5 - Always expressed feeling

Mother	Father	Feeling	Self
2	5	Anger	1
		Anger	
		Humor	
		Warmth	
		Sadness	
		Patience	
		Frustration	
		Fear	
		Violence	
		Jealousy	
		Embarrassment	
		Hurt	
		Understanding	
		Shame	
		Worry	
		Guilt	
		Confusion	
		Moodiness	
		Nurturance	

Mother

Select six feelings that describe your mother's expression of feelings and give a reason for your rating.

Example:

_____ Anger _____ 2 _____ My mother was over-powered by my dad's anger and rarely expressed her feelings, especially anger.

Feeling   Rating   Rationale

1. _____

_____

_____

_____

2. _____

_____

_____

_____

3. _____

_____

_____

4. _____

_____

_____

_____

5. _____

_____

_____

_____

6. _____

_____

_____

Father

Select six feelings that describe your father's expression of feelings and give a reason for your rating.

Feeling   Rating   Rationale

1. _____

_____

_____

_____

_____

2. _____

_____

_____

_____

_____

3. _____

_____

_____

_____

4. _____

_____

_____

_____

_____

5. _____

_____

_____

_____

6. _____

_____

_____

_____

PART TWO
Feelings Today

Self

Select six feelings that describe your expression of feelings and give a reason for your rating.

Feeling   Rating   Rationale

1. _____

_____

_____

_____

2. _____

_____

_____

_____

3. _____

_____

_____

_____

_____

4. _____

_____

_____

_____

_____

5. _____

_____

_____

_____

6. _____

_____

_____

_____

Today

Comment on how your parents' expression of their own feelings toward or around you as a child affects you today.

_____

_____

_____

_____

_____

_____

_____

_____

_____

_____

_____

_____

_____

_____

_____

_____

_____

_____

_____

_____

_____

_____

_____

_____

_____

_____

_____

The Cat Family Story

TITLE: _____

GIVE THE NAMES AND AGES OF ALL THE CATS
INVOLVED IN THE SCENE:

_____ _____ _____

_____ _____ _____

 WHERE IS THE SCENE TAKING PLACE?

_____

WHAT LED UP TO THIS SCENE?

_____

_____

_____

_____

_____

_____

_____

_____

_____

TELL WHY THE CATS ARE DOING WHAT THEY
ARE DOING

_____

_____

_____

_____

_____

_____

_____

_____

_____

_____

_____

WHAT IS THE OUTCOME OF THE STORY?

_____

_____

_____

_____

_____

_____

_____

_____

_____

_____

_____

_____

_____

_____

NOTES

CHAPTER FIVE

ANGER

Anger is a feeling that everyone experiences in day-to-day living. Many Children of Alcoholics claim to feel numb or no anger at all. Many of us feel a tremendous fear of our anger or explode into rages. We often saw our parents either express anger inappropriately (e.g., beating their children, kicking the dog, putting a fist through the wall) or not express anger at all, especially in situations when feeling angry would have been appropriate.

Holding anger in distorts and twists our feelings inside so that when it is released, it comes out distorted and twisted. We may even deny our angry feelings, especially toward our parents.

In general, there are three ways that Children of Alcoholics express anger: Exploding, Sideswiping or Stuffing.

Exploders: Often go into rages over insignificant things and act calm over issues in which anger would be appropriate; often punish anyone in their path, either physically or verbally.

Possible Consequences: Low self-esteem, loss of friends and family, self-debasement or problems with the law or authority.

Sideswipers: Often use passive-aggressive techniques, seek revenge and avoid direct confrontations; often punish others through martyrdom and verbal abuse.

Possible Consequences: Low self-esteem, martyrdom, illusion of power over others; rejection or physical illness.

Stuffers: Often hold in and stuff angry or hurt feelings; often punish self through self-destructive measures; often punish others by withdrawing into self.

Possible Consequences: Low self-esteem, martyrdom, isolation, physical illness and suicidal feelings.

*THE **EXPRESSION** OF ANGER IS LEARNED BEHAVIOR. THE FEELING OF ANGER IS HUMAN. AS A CHILD OF AN ALCOHOLIC, YOU MAY HAVE LEARNED TO EXPRESS YOUR ANGER LIKE ONE OR BOTH OF YOUR PARENTS. EXAMINING YOUR PARENTS' AND YOUR OWN EXPRESSION OF ANGER MAY AID YOU IN SELF-UNDERSTANDING AND COMPASSION. YOU MAY ALSO BEGIN TO SEE CHOICES IN TERMS OF EXPRESSING YOUR ANGRY FEELINGS.*

PART ONE
Expression of Anger

Mother

Describe three ways your mother showed her anger:

(e.g., drinking too much, slamming kitchen cabinet doors, silent treatment.)

1. _____

_____

2. _____

_____

3. _____

_____

Father

Describe three ways your father showed his anger:

(e.g., driving his car too fast and yelling at other drivers, beating my mother, drinking too much.)

1. _____

_____

2. _____

_____

3. _____

_____

PART TWO
Today

Describe three ways you show your anger today:

(e.g., hitting walls, breaking windows, yelling at other drivers.)

1. _____

_____

2. _____

_____

3. _____

_____

Which of the three ways of expressing anger do you identify with the most?

_____ Exploder

_____ Sideswiper

_____ Stuffer

I express anger most like:

_____ Mother

_____ Father

_____ Both

Are you afraid you will get out of control if you get angry?

_____ Yes

_____ No

_____ Sometimes

PART THREE
History

Describe your anger history. Include:

1. **Messages:** Describe the messages you received from your parents and siblings about expressing anger.

2. **Behavior:** Describe how family members expressed anger. Include the kinds of situations in which it was appropriate to express anger.

3. **Ability:** Describe your ability to express your angry feelings. Include your ability to say "No" when you want to.

(e.g. **Childhood** (0–10 Years): It was generally said that raising your voice was wrong and that getting angry would lead to sin. "Who do you think you are to raise your voice to me—go to your room and don't come out until you can act like a good boy should." Showing anger or even mild dissatisfaction was chastised. My father was the only one who expressed anger. He seemed to be angry at the whole world. The rest of us got out of his way when he would get mad—which was most of the time. My mother expressed anger in the name of making us "good little Christians." She was sadistic at times. She didn't allow us to be angry or loud. I learned early to not get angry—at least I never showed it. I was very tough and could take it. I never said "No" to my parents. I learned to say "Yes" with a smile, even when I felt furious inside. Often I would just feel numb.)

Childhood (0–10 Years) _____

_____

_____

_____

_____

_____

_____

_____

Adolescence (10–17 Years) _____

_____

_____

_____

_____

_____

_____

Adulthood (17 Years and Older) _____

_____

_____

_____

_____

_____

_____

PART FOUR
Feelings

Look at the feelings list and identify three feelings that you have about your anger history and explain.

(e.g., **SAD**—I feel sad because I have hurt others with my explosive temper, especially people I love.)

1. I feel _____ because _____

_____

_____

_____

_____

_____

2. I feel _____ because _____

_____

_____

_____

_____

_____

3. I feel _____ because _____

_____

_____

_____

_____

_____

_____

_____

The Cat Family Story

TITLE: _____

GIVE THE NAMES AND AGES OF ALL THE CATS
INVOLVED IN THE SCENE:

_____ _____ _____

_____ _____ _____

WHERE IS THE SCENE TAKING PLACE?

_____

WHAT LED UP TO THIS SCENE?

_____

_____

_____

_____

_____

_____

_____

_____

_____

_____

_____

_____

TELL WHY THE CATS ARE DOING WHAT THEY
ARE DOING

_____

_____

_____

_____

_____

_____

_____

_____

_____

_____

_____

_____

_____

WHAT IS THE OUTCOME OF THE STORY?

_____

_____

_____

_____

_____

_____

_____

_____

_____

_____

_____

_____

NOTES

CHAPTER SIX

FEAR

Fear is a natural reaction to many situations that Children of Alcoholics face in their childhood. Many times, it is difficult for us to identify exactly what we fear, especially when things appear to be calm. There may be other times when we have no fear at all, even when it is appropriate to feel fear in certain situations.

Many of us are afraid to express our needs for fear of losing love. Many of us are fearful of criticism, disagreements or misunderstandings. To avoid criticism or humiliation, we attempted to anticipate our parents' wants or needs. Sometimes our radar worked; however, sometimes it didn't. In some families, a disagreement often resulted in loud arguing and name calling or physical violence.

Many of us experienced fear of the unknown, never knowing what to expect next. This may be expressed in "what if" fears today. **"What if the car breaks down." "What if he doesn't show up." "What if I'm alone forever."**

FOR MANY CHILDREN OF ALCOHOLICS, IDENTIFYING YOUR REAL AND IMAGINED FEARS MAY HELP YOU TO BE RELEASED FROM THEM. FEARS BECOME MORE POWERFUL WHEN THEY ARE NOT EXPRESSED.

PART ONE
Rituals and Routines

1. What were your fears about mealtimes in your family?

(e.g., I feared that my parents would fight and my dad would leave.)

I feared _____

_____

_____

_____

_____

This happened:

Often _____ Rarely _____ Never _____

2. What were your fears about bedtime?

(e.g. I feared that my father would tuck me in and touch me.)

I feared _____

_____

_____

_____

_____

This happened:

Often _____ Rarely _____ Never _____

3. What were your fears about school?

(e.g. I feared that I wouldn't get good enough grades to please my mom.)

I feared _____

_____

_____

This happened:

Often _____ Rarely _____ Never _____

4. What were your fears about holidays and birthdays? (e.g. I feared that my parents would get drunk at the bar and leave us kids alone.)

I feared _____

_____

_____

_____

_____

This happened:

Often _____ Rarely _____ Never _____

PART TWO
Behavior

Answer the following by circling Y (Yes), N (No), or S (Sometimes).

Did you fear that your parents were going to abandon you or leave you for extended periods uncared for?

Y   N   S

Were you often afraid that you were going to be hit for no reason?

Y   N   S

Were you afraid that your mother did not love you?

Y   N   S

Were you afraid that your father did not love you?

Y   N   S

Name three things you did when you felt fearful as a child. (e.g., hid in my closet, ran away, sucked my thumb.)

1. _____

_____

2. _____

_____

3. _____

_____

PART THREE
Today

Do you pretend today that you're not afraid when you really are?

Y   N   S

Is there anyone you can tell when you feel afraid?

Y   N   S

Who? _____

Identify three fears you have today.

(e.g., fear of sexual intimacy, fear of my partner's anger, fear of flying in an airplane.)

1. _____

_____

2. _____

_____

3. _____

_____

Describe how each fear is in your way of feeling free or fulfilled today.

(e.g., **Fear of Sexual Intimacy:** I have a difficult time being sexual. I often enjoy sex after I'm involved in it, but I avoid my partner's advances. I often feel physically shut down. My partners *always* feel blamed for my disinterest. I feel guilty and stuck. It seems to be connected to being molested by my stepfather as a child. He was an alcoholic.)

1. Fear: _____

_____

_____

_____

_____

_____

_____

_____

_____

_____

_____

_____

_____

_____

_____

_____

_____

2. Fear: _____

_____

_____

_____

_____

_____

_____

_____

_____

_____

_____

_____

_____

_____

_____

3. Fear: _____

_____

_____

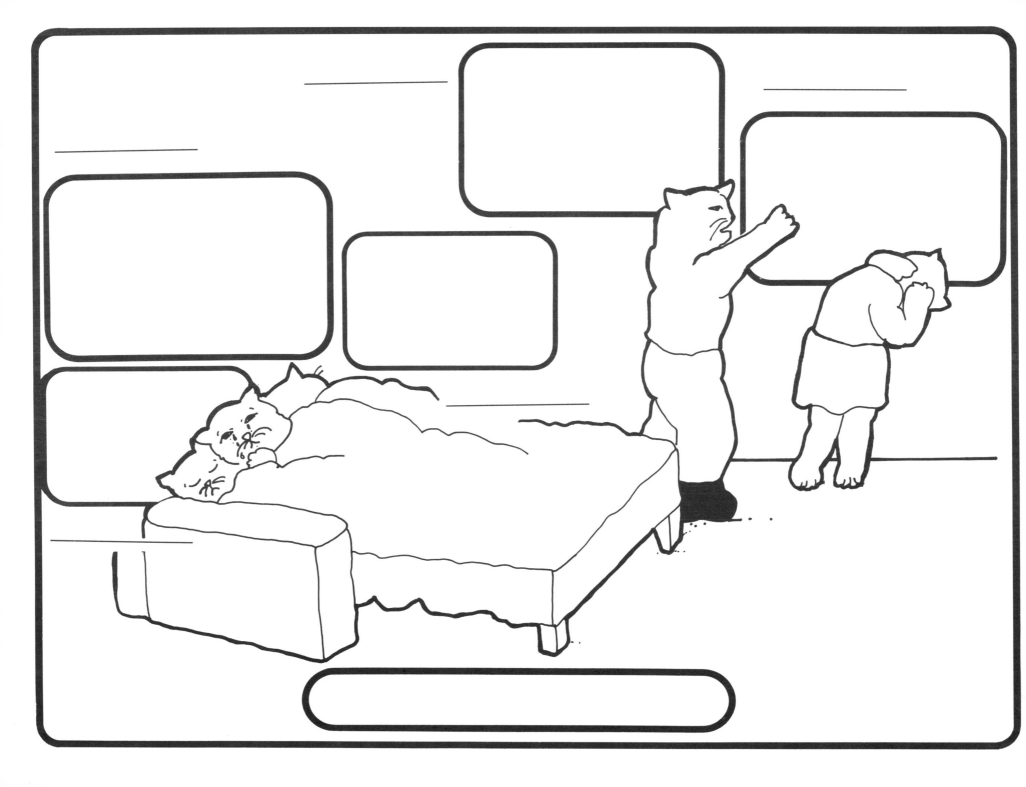

The Cat Family Story

TITLE: _____

GIVE THE NAMES AND AGES OF ALL THE CATS INVOLVED IN THE SCENE:

_____ _____ _____

_____ _____ _____

WHERE IS THE SCENE TAKING PLACE?

_____

WHAT LED UP TO THIS SCENE?

_____

_____

_____

_____

_____

_____

_____

_____

_____

TELL WHY THE CATS ARE DOING WHAT THEY ARE DOING

_____

_____

_____

_____

_____

_____

_____

_____

_____

_____

_____

_____

_____

WHAT IS THE OUTCOME OF THE STORY?

NOTES

CHAPTER SEVEN
SHAME & GUILT

Many Children of Alcoholics believe that their behavior, and sometimes even their existence, can cause their parents to drink. Many alcoholic parents blame their children and spouse for causing them to drink. "You drive me to drink" or "If it wasn't for you kids, I wouldn't get upset and I wouldn't have to drink" are a couple of common shame and guilt inducers that we heard throughout our childhood. For many of us, knowing that we don't cause our parents to drink, and especially that we can't cure them, is important, but it doesn't take away the shame and guilt feelings.

Shame is the feeling that Children of Alcoholics take on to make sense of the dysfunctional behavior of our parents. We took responsibility for their actions rather than feel the tremendous pain of their abuse or abandonment. An example of child-like thinking is "It must be my fault that my parents don't like me. There's something wrong with me."

Many parents from alcoholic families use shame and guilt to control or manipulate their children. Shame Inducers may be non-verbal or verbal, direct or indirect messages. Whatever form they take, the effect is often the same; shame inducers affect our behavior and decisions as adults.

Guilt is the feeling that Children of Alcoholics feel when we cause injuries to ourselves or others due to our own actions. Taking responsibility for our own dysfunctional behavior is an important part of our recovery process.

IDENTIFYING THE SHAME INDUCERS YOUR PARENTS USED OR CONTINUE TO USE TODAY WILL BE THE FIRST STEP IN RELEASING SHAME. ALLOW SELF-FORGIVENESS TO EMERGE AS YOU LET GO OF GUILT AND CHOOSE NEW FUNCTIONAL BEHAVIORS THAT COME FROM YOUR TRUE SELF INSTEAD OF REACTIONS TO OUR PARENTS' BEHAVIOR AND EXPECTATIONS.

PART ONE
Shame Inducers

Mother

Identify three Shame Inducers that your mother used or continues to use today to control, humiliate or manipulate you. (e.g., 1. A look of desperation followed by tears if I don't go along with her ideas for me; 2. Comments like "Your father gives me enough trouble – now you. How can you do this to me."; 3. A lecture about the proper way to act.)

1. Shame Inducers: _____

_____

_____

_____

_____

_____

_____

2. Shame Inducers: _____

_____

_____

_____

_____

_____

_____

_____

_____

3. Shame Inducers: _____

_____

_____

_____

_____

_____

_____

Father

Identify three Shame Inducers that your father used or continues to use today to control, humiliate or manipulate you. (e.g., 1. Comments like "What's wrong with you?"; 2. Hostile and rejecting looks; 3. Comments like "Who do you think you are?")

1. Shame Inducers: _____

_____

_____

_____

_____

_____

_____

_____

2. Shame Inducers: _____

_____

_____

_____

_____

_____

_____

_____

3. Shame Inducers: _____

_____

_____

_____

_____

_____

_____

_____

_____

_____

Behavior

Identify three behaviors you developed in response to Shame Inducers (e.g., nailbiting, people pleasing, breaking the rules on purpose.)

1. _____

_____

2. _____

_____

3. _____

_____

PART TWO

Secret Guilts

Identify your secret guilts from your childhood, adolescence and adulthood that you continue to carry with you today. These secret guilts may not necessarily be ones that you've kept only to yourself but those that you feel embarrassed to share with others. They may be actions that are a result of poor judgement due to the effects of growing up in an alcoholic home.

Childhood (0-10 Years) (e.g., I slapped my little sister around and would deny it to my parents.)

1. _____

_____

_____

_____

2. _____

_____

_____

_____

3. _____

_____

_____

_____

Adolescence (10-17 Years) (e.g., I stole money from my father's wallet whenever he was drunk.)

1. _____

_____

_____

2. _____

_____

_____

3. _____

_____

_____

Adulthood (17 Years and Older) (e.g., I cheated my business partner out of money.)

1. _____

_____

_____

2. _____

_____

_____

3. _____

_____

_____

_____

PART THREE
Forgiveness

Rewrite all of the above secret guilts, and at the end of each statement write, **"I FORGIVE MYSELF TODAY."** (e.g., I slapped my little sister around and denied it to my parents – I FORGIVE MYSELF TODAY.) You may not feel self forgiveness as you're rewriting these statements. Notice your emotional snags and let awareness release you of shame and guilt.

1. _____

_____

_____

_____

_____

_____

_____

2. _____

_____

_____

_____

_____

_____

3. _____

_____

_____

_____

_____

_____

4. _____

_____

_____

_____

_____

_____

_____

_____

_____

5. _____

_____

_____

_____

_____

6. _____

_____

_____

_____

7. _____

_____

_____

_____

_____

_____

_____

_____

8. _____

_____

_____

_____

_____

_____

9. _____

_____

_____

_____

The Cat Family Story

TITLE: _____

GIVE THE NAMES AND AGES OF ALL THE CATS
INVOLVED IN THE SCENE:

_____ _____ _____

_____ _____ _____

WHERE IS THE SCENE TAKING PLACE?

_____

WHAT LED UP TO THIS SCENE?

_____

_____

_____

_____

_____

_____

_____

_____

_____

_____

_____

_____

_____

TELL WHY THE CATS ARE DOING WHAT THEY
ARE DOING

_____

_____

_____

_____

_____

_____

_____

_____

_____

_____

_____

_____

WHAT IS THE OUTCOME OF THE STORY?

_____

_____

_____

_____

_____

_____

_____

_____

_____

_____

_____

_____

_____

_____

_____

_____

_____

_____

_____

_____

_____

_____

_____

_____

NOTES

CHAPTER EIGHT
CRYING

Crying is a natural release for emotions. It is normal to cry when we feel sad, lonely, scared, happy, etc. In other words, crying comes with feeling our feelings. Sometimes parents have a difficult time seeing their children cry. They may give their children unhealthy messages like, **"You're oversensitive." "Don't be such a crybaby." "I'll give you something to cry about."** These messages may be given because the parent may feel guilty about their drinking or their spouse's drinking and how it affects their children.

Some of us stopped crying or showing our feelings or hurt when we realized that our parents were not there for us or our needs. It doesn't take long before we stop knocking on our parents' "emotional door" for comfort or understanding. In fact, in many alcoholic families, we were rewarded and complimented for meeting our own needs and for not bothering our preoccupied parents with "childish" requests. Many of us can remember a conscious decision made at a very young age that we would no longer cry or show emotion. Our vulnerability and pain would be hidden from view.

TELLING YOU, WHETHER WITH WORDS OR A MEAN LOOK, NOT TO FEEL OR EXPRESS YOUR FEELINGS MAY HAVE HAD AN EFFECT ON YOUR ABILITY TO CRY TODAY. LOOKING AT PARENTAL MESSAGES ABOUT CRYING MAY HELP YOU TO CHANGE THOSE MESSAGES TODAY AND ALLOW THE TEARS TO FLOW.

PART ONE
Expression of Sadness or Hurt
Mother

Identify three situations in which your mother openly expressed sadness or hurt by crying. (e.g. After the police took my father away because of violence, my mother broke down and cried. She let me hold her. I felt so needed. I was nine years old.)

1. _____

_____

_____

_____

_____

2. _____

_____

_____

_____

3. _____

_____

_____

_____

_____

_____

Father

Identify three situations in which your father openly expressed sadness or hurt by crying. (e.g. I saw my father cry when his mother died. He tried to hide his pain but he couldn't.)

1. _____

_____

_____

_____

2. _____

_____

_____

_____

3. _____

_____

_____

_____

PART TWO
Today

Take a look at how you've learned to express or deny your feelings, especially your tears, by answering the following questions. Answer by circling Y (Yes), N (No), or S (Sometimes).

Are you able to cry?

        Y   N   S

Do you cry only when you are alone?

        Y   N   S

Are you able to cry when your feelings are hurt by others?

        Y   N   S

Do you cry for no reason?

        Y   N   S

Are you able to let others know when you cry?

        Y   N   S

Are you able to let others comfort or hold you when you cry?

        Y   N   S

Do you feel angry at yourself for crying, especially in front of others?

        Y   N   S

Do you cry when you are angry?

        Y   N   S

Name three ways in which you resist crying today:
(e.g. leave the situation, move or fidget to distract myself from my feelings, swallow hard and hold them back.)

1. _____

_____

2. _____

_____

3. _____

_____

PART THREE
History

Describe your crying history and ability to cry. Include:

Messages: Describe the messages you received from your parents or siblings about crying.

Behavior: Describe how often you and other family members cried.

Ability: Describe the kinds of situations in which it was appropriate to cry. Describe your ability to cry. Do you experience delayed feelings or tears?

For example: **Childhood** (0–10 years) My mother did not like anyone to cry. She often said, "I'll give you something to cry about." This taught me early on not to cry, at least in front of her. She seemed to be the only one who could cry. I often felt embarrassed by her range of emotions, especially when she would break down in front of anyone outside of the family. It was okay to cry briefly over physical pain—it was *not* okay to cry over emotional pain. "You're being silly." I rarely could cry in the moment. I often felt sad or tearful but hid it till I was alone.)

Childhood (0–10 years) _____

_____

_____

_____

_____

_____

_____

_____

_____

_____

_____

_____

Adolescence (10–17 years) _____

_____

Adulthood (17 years and older) _____

The Cat Family Story

TITLE: _____

GIVE THE NAMES AND AGES OF ALL THE CATS INVOLVED IN THE SCENE:

_____ _____ _____

_____ _____ _____

WHERE IS THE SCENE TAKING PLACE?

_____

WHAT LED UP TO THIS SCENE?

_____

_____

_____

_____

_____

_____

_____

_____

_____

TELL WHY THE CATS ARE DOING WHAT THEY ARE DOING

_____

_____

_____

_____

_____

_____

_____

_____

_____

_____

_____

_____

WHAT IS THE OUTCOME OF THE STORY?

_____

_____

_____

_____

_____

_____

_____

_____

_____

_____

_____

_____

_____

_____

_____

_____

_____

_____

_____

_____

_____

_____

_____

_____

NOTES

CHAPTER NINE

GRIEF

Many Children of Alcoholics have experienced losses which have been overwhelming. You may have lost a parent to death, alcoholism, mental illness, divorce, or abandonment. You may have lost your childhood to trying to survive or to caring for out-of-control adults around you. As a result, some of us decide to avoid situations or people that remind us of our pain or losses. We also avoid intimate friendships or relationships in an attempt to minimize the possibility of more loss or abandonment in our life.

There are five stages of Grief.

Denial - "Nothing is wrong." "I don't feel anything." "I don't care."

Anger - "I hate her anyway." "I don't care about him."

Bargaining - "Maybe she'll change." "Maybe they'll get it together soon."

Depression - "I feel sad." "I can't do anything but sleep." "I feel scared and lonely."

Acceptance - "I can see now what it's all about." "I feel relieved." "I can accept things as they are—not as I'd like them to be."

Some of us get stuck in the first three stages, which prevents us from growing up emotionally and from opening the door to our heart to new people or new experiences.

TALKING ABOUT YOUR LOSSES, YOUR FEELINGS AND YOUR PAIN WILL HELP YOU GO THROUGH THE STAGES OF GRIEF.

PART ONE
The Losses

List three family members or friends that you lost to death, alcoholism, mental illness, abandonment, or separation:

Name of Family Member or Friend   **Identify Means of Loss**

e.g.   Dad   My parents divorced when I was 2. I felt abandoned by my Dad.

1. _____   _____

_____

_____

_____

2. _____   _____

_____

_____

_____

3. _____   _____

_____

_____

_____

PART TWO
Real and Ideal

Using the feeling list, identify your real and ideal feelings about your family members or friend from Part One. Your ideal feelings may be the ones that you wish you felt for your family member or friend.

**Real Feelings
for Family / Friend**

For example:

Name: Dad
Anger
Disappointed
Blamed

**Ideal Feelings
for Family / Friend**

Name: Dad
Caring
Nurturance
Love

1. **Name:** _____

_____

_____

_____

2. **Name:** _____

_____

_____

_____

3. **Name:** _____

_____

_____

_____

Name: _____

_____

_____

_____

Name: _____

_____

_____

_____

Name: _____

_____

_____

_____

PART THREE
Stages of Grief

Review the five stages of Grief. Identify which Stage of Grief you are in for each family member or friend from Part Two.

(e.g., Dad—Stage of **Bargaining** because I think that maybe if I'm perfect, he'll come back. I am still lonely for a father figure and try to get older men in my life to be a father to me.)

1. _____ Stage of _____ because

_____

_____

_____

_____

_____

2. _____ Stage of _____ because

_____

_____

_____

_____

3. _____ Stage of _____ because _____

_____

_____

_____

_____

_____

_____

PART FOUR
Today

Select one of the three family members or friend from Part Three and describe in detail your feelings regarding your loss and how this loss affects you today.

_____

_____

_____

_____

_____

_____

_____

_____

_____

_____

_____

_____

_____

_____

_____

_____

_____

_____

_____

_____

_____

_____

_____

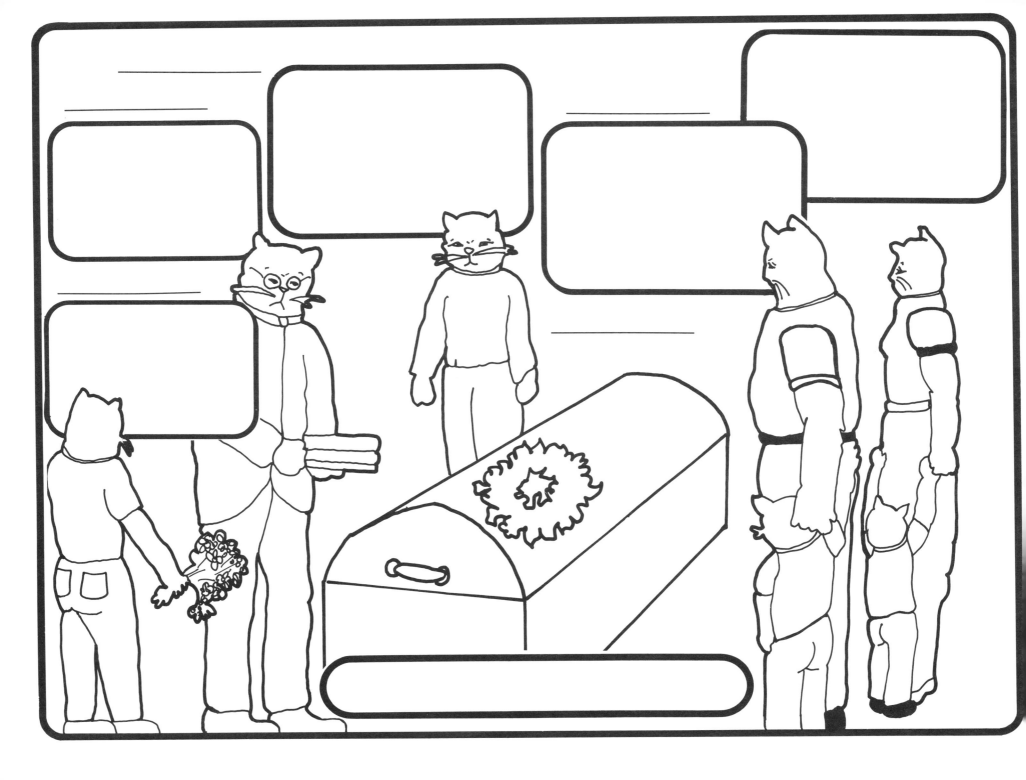

The Cat Family Story

TITLE: _____

GIVE THE NAMES AND AGES OF ALL THE CATS INVOLVED IN THE SCENE:

_____   _____   _____

_____   _____   _____

WHERE IS THE SCENE TAKING PLACE?

_____

WHAT LED UP TO THIS SCENE?

_____

_____

_____

_____

_____

_____

_____

_____

TELL WHY THE CATS ARE DOING WHAT THEY ARE DOING

_____

_____

_____

_____

_____

_____

_____

_____

_____

_____

_____

WHAT IS THE OUTCOME OF THE STORY?

NOTES

CHAPTER TEN

SEX ROLES

Many Children of Alcoholics grow up in families where sex role expectations are very rigid or limiting. This often affects our expression of feelings and behavior, especially feelings and behavior associated with the opposite sex. Often we are confused by our parents' attitudes about femininity and masculinity. Many times what they said about being a man or a woman contradicted their behavior.

In many alcoholic families, parental role models are abusive and tyrannical or weak and incompetent. Many of us secretly hope that we will never be like our parents. We may choose to reject our parents' modeling of adult behavior or completely accept their values and behavioral expectations in reaction to the dysfunction of the family. Many of us learned social skills and values outside of the family. This may have been due to parental absence or negative role modeling by parents. The result was often confusion and frustration for us as Children of Alcoholics. Many of us find that our efforts to be "different" than our parents are not met with positive results; often Children of Alcoholics either marry alcoholics, become alcoholics themselves, or both. In alcoholic families, there are many unspoken rules about feelings and behavior. These unspoken rules are powerful and often influence our choices.

BECOMING AWARE OF YOUR FEELINGS IS AN ESSENTIAL STEP TOWARDS RECOVERY. ANOTHER STEP IS TO IDENTIFY FEELINGS YOU DON'T EXPERIENCE, DUE TO UNSPOKEN FAMILY RULES ABOUT SHOWING FEELINGS, ESPECIALLY THOSE FEELINGS TYPICALLY ASSOCIATED WITH THE OPPOSITE SEX.

PART ONE
Feelings

Many Children of Alcoholics have attitudes and values about expression of feelings based on sex due to growing up in their alcoholic family. These attitudes and values that you learned as a child may continue to effect your expression of feelings today. These attitudes and values may also effect how you view men and women.

Identify feelings that men generally have access to or express based on your family attitudes and values by placing an **M** next to those feelings. Identify feelings that women generally have access to or express based on your family attitudes and values by placing a **W** next to those feelings.

Anger	_____	Happy	_____
Guilt	_____	Sad	_____
Worry	_____	Disappointed	_____
Hurt	_____	Rejected	_____
Confused	_____	Abandoning	_____
Curious	_____	Bored	_____
Hopeless	_____	Blamed	_____
Hopeful	_____	Betrayed	_____
Pressured	_____	Shy	_____
Sure	_____	Embarrassed	_____
Satisfied	_____	Caring	_____
Joy	_____	Trapped	_____
Scared	_____	Mean	_____
Hostile	_____	Confident	_____
Tender	_____	Carefree	_____

Men

Select five feelings that men mostly feel and explain.

(e.g., satisfied — Men feel more satisfied with their life than women because they are not burdened with children or household chores.)

1. _____

_____

_____

_____

2. _____

_____

_____

_____

3. _____

_____

_____

_____

4. _____

_____

_____

_____

5. _____

_____

_____

_____

Women

Select five feelings that women mostly feel and explain.

(e.g., worry—Women feel worried because they can't control their spouses' behavior or drinking.

1. _____

_____

_____

_____

2. _____

_____

_____

_____

3. _____

_____

_____

_____

4. _____

_____

_____

_____

5. _____

_____

_____

_____

PART TWO
Today

Rewrite the five feelings of your sex by owning the feelings.

(e.g., I feel worried because I can't control my spouse's behavior or drinking.)

1. _____

_____

_____

_____

2. _____

_____

_____

_____

3. _____

_____

_____

4. _____

_____

_____

_____

5. _____

_____

_____

_____

Comment on whether some or all of the rewritten sentences are accurate for you.

_____

_____

_____

_____

_____

_____

_____

_____

_____

PART THREE
Expectations

Comment on how you were affected by sex role expectations in your family. Include:

1. **Messages**—Messages you received from parents and siblings about sex roles and expressing feelings.

   (e.g., mostly my parents wanted me to act like a grown-up. That meant that I shouldn't express feelings, especially sad feelings. My siblings teased me if I cried, so I stopped. "Boys don't cry. They are supposed to get mad."

2. **Behavior**—Describe how family members expressed their sex role identification. Also describe the kinds of behaviors that were appropriate or inappropriate for your sex, according to your family.

   (e.g., My mom tried to act feminine, but with Dad drunk or gone so much, she was often tough on us and acted like an army drill sergeant. Dad was angry in a quiet way. He'd just punish us by drinking. When he got drunk, he was withdrawn and rejecting. Being a boy, I wasn't allowed to cry, but I wasn't allowed to be strong either—like making decisions for myself or going out by myself. My sisters were treated like servants. They did all the housework. They resented me sometimes and took out their anger towards my mom and dad on me. I knew I didn't want to be like my Dad, but I didn't know who to be like. I decided to be opposite of him, but unfortunately, that didn't work either.)

The Cat Family Story

TITLE: _____

GIVE THE NAMES AND AGES OF ALL THE CATS INVOLVED IN THE SCENE:

_____ _____ _____

_____ _____ _____

WHERE IS THE SCENE TAKING PLACE?

_____

WHAT LED UP TO THIS SCENE?

_____

_____

_____

_____

_____

_____

_____

_____

_____

_____

_____

_____

_____

TELL WHY THE CATS ARE DOING WHAT THEY ARE DOING

_____

_____

_____

_____

_____

_____

_____

_____

_____

_____

_____

WHAT IS THE OUTCOME OF THE STORY?

_____

_____

_____

_____

_____

_____

_____

_____

_____

_____

_____

_____

_____

_____

_____

_____

_____

_____

_____

_____

_____

_____

_____

_____

_____

_____

NOTES

CHAPTER ELEVEN

RELATIONSHIPS

Generally, our behavior and attitudes as Children of Alcoholics are developed in reaction to our alcoholic and co-dependent parents. Some of us are a lot like our parents, while others rebel against what our parents are like and attempt to be the opposite. The differences between Children of Alcoholics and their parents are often superficial. Feelings are often the same in adulthood as they were as a child in relation to parents and to oneself.

Many Children of Alcoholics experience an inability to be intimate, which is often confused with a lack of interest or desire. Parallel existence in relationships is very common for us; each partner functioning separately with little or no emotional or sexual intimacy.

Other Children of Alcoholics choose conflictual relationships that may resemble our parents relationship. Our ability to cope with and accept the unacceptable is extraordinary; therefore, many of us grow to accept lifelong misery and unacceptable treatment.

THE MESSAGES YOUR PARENTS GAVE YOU ABOUT RELATIONSHIPS AND THE WAY THEY TREATED EACH OTHER AND YOU HAVE INFLUENCED YOUR CHOICES AND FEELINGS TODAY, ESPECIALLY IN INTIMATE RELATIONSHIPS. EXAMINING YOUR PARENTS' RELATIONSHIP AND ATTITUDES MAY ASSIST YOU IN UNDERSTANDING YOUR OWN.

PART ONE
Generational Relationships

Mother

Describe the kind of relationship your mother had with her parents.

(e.g. Mother -	My mom hated her mother. She criticized her whenever I asked about her. She felt like her mother rejected her.
Father	My mom liked her father. She did say he drank a lot but that he gave her a lot of attention and presents. She felt like her father loved her, especially when her mother was picking on her.)

My mother's feeling about her own mother were/

are: _____

_____

_____

_____

_____

My mother's feeling about her father were/are: ___

_____

_____

_____

_____

_____

_____

Father

Describe the kind of relationship your father had with his parents.

(e.g. Mother -   My dad never talked about his mother.
                        She left him when he was six years
                        old. He won't see her or talk about
                        her.

Father   My dad hated his father and left home
                        as soon as he could. He doesn't seem
                        to be close to any of his relatives.)

My father's feeling about his own mother were/

are: _____

_____

_____

_____

_____

My father's feeling about his own father were/are:

_____

_____

_____

_____

_____

_____

PART TWO
Parents' Relationship

What kind of marriage do you think your parents had? Select one and explain.

    1. Loving
    2. Hurtful
    3. Mostly Loving, but Sometimes Hurtful
    4. Mostly Hurtful, but Sometimes Loving

(e.g., **Hurtful** because they seemed to fight or give each other the silent treatment a lot. They never showed each other affection like hugging or kissing in front of us kids. My dad was depressed a lot and my mom was trying to get his attention by yelling at him.)

_____

because _____

_____

_____

_____

_____

_____

_____

_____

_____

_____

PART THREE
Responsibility

Mother

Describe your parent's attitudes or feelings about whether you were a planned and wanted baby.

(e.g. My mother often said it was a big mistake to have child (me) when she knew she wanted to leave my dad. She felt trapped.)

Mother: _____

_____

_____

_____

_____

_____

_____

_____

_____

Father

(e.g. My father was cold and detached. We just never felt close. I think he blamed me for his choice to stay married to my mother.)

Father: _____

_____

_____

_____

_____

_____

Did you feel responsible for the problems your parents had with each other? If so, how were you responsible?

(e.g., I felt responsible because my parents mostly fought about money and me. I thought my dad's drinking was due to his loss of freedom at a young age and bad luck with jobs and employers. I didn't realize that the money problems were due to his drinking. As for me, my parents got married young, even though they didn't want to, because my mom got pregnant with me. I felt that their problems would disappear if it wasn't for me. At 15, I ran away from home and didn't see them again until I was 24. Not much had changed.)

I felt responsible because _____

_____

_____

_____

_____

_____

_____

_____

_____

_____

_____

Behavior

Name three ways you tried to win your parent's love, attention, or approval.

(e.g., getting straight A's in school, acting out in school, staying out of their way and not asking for help.)

1. _____

_____

2. _____

_____

3. _____

_____

PART FOUR
Relationships Today

What kind of intimate relationship do you often have? Select one and explain.

1. Loving
2. Hurtful
3. Mostly Loving, but Sometimes Hurtful
4. Mostly Hurtful, but Sometimes Loving

_____

because _____

_____

_____

_____

_____

_____

_____

Select three feelings from the feeling list to describe how you feel in intimate relationships.

(e.g., I feel trapped because the people I choose are demanding and critical and I'm afraid to leave them. I don't like being alone.)

1. I feel _____ because _____

_____

_____

_____

_____

2. I feel _____ because _____

_____

_____

_____

_____

_____

_____

_____

3. I feel _____ because _____

_____

_____

_____

_____

_____

_____

_____

_____

PART FIVE
Ideal Relationship

Describe your **ideal** intimate relationship. Be descriptive and creative. Include emotional, intellectual, sexual, spiritual and communication ideals.

_____

_____

_____

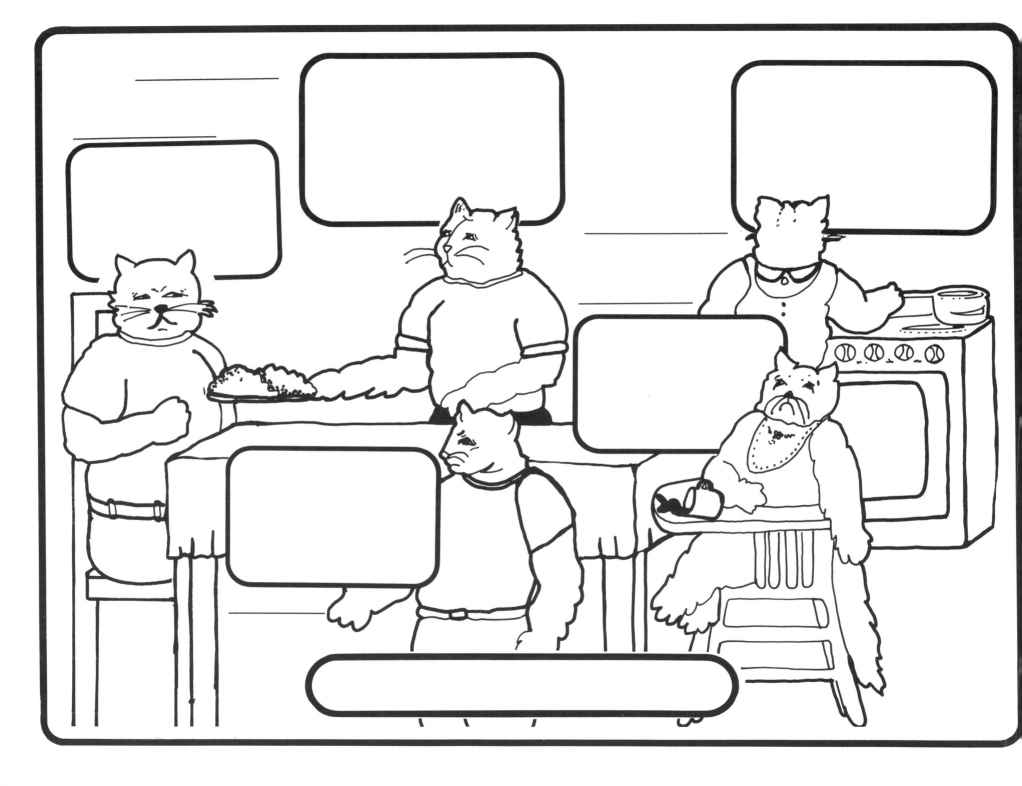

The Cat Family Story

TITLE: _____

GIVE THE NAMES AND AGES OF ALL THE CATS
INVOLVED IN THE SCENE:

_____ _____ _____

_____ _____ _____

WHERE IS THE SCENE TAKING PLACE?

WHAT LED UP TO THIS SCENE?

_____

_____

_____

_____

_____

_____

_____

_____

_____

_____

_____

_____

TELL WHY THE CATS ARE DOING WHAT THEY
ARE DOING

_____

_____

_____

_____

_____

_____

_____

_____

_____

_____

_____

_____

WHAT IS THE OUTCOME OF THE STORY?

NOTES

CHAPTER TWELVE

PARENTS

Children of Alcoholics experience pain and loss in relation to our parents due to alcoholism, separation, divorce, or emotional abandonment. Some of us grew up with stepparents. This can be very confusing and awkward. Family roles may not have been clear. We often act out the role of the absent parent, wanting to protect our other parent, or feeling like we didn't need anyone else in the household telling us what to do.

Some of us have difficulty seeing our parents as they really are. Often we see them as horrible, cruel, and unloving, or as wonderful, gentle, and loving. Generally, what is true is often a combination of both. Most of us prefer to forget or deny that our parents have hurt us or made mistakes. Others blame all their problems on their parents. Again, what's true is often a combination of both.

MATURING EMOTIONALLY INCLUDES CONFRONTING OUR REAL FEELINGS ABOUT OUR PARENTS. YOUR CHILDHOOD EXPERIENCES AND THE FEELINGS ASSOCIATED WITH THOSE EXPERIENCES IN RELATION TO YOUR PARENTS MAY ASSIST YOU IN DEVELOPING A CLEARER UNDERSTANDING OF YOURSELF AND YOUR REACTIONS IN GENERAL AND SPECIFICALLY TOWARDS YOUR PARENTS.

PART ONE
Feelings

Mother

Identify three feelings you have for your mother from the feeling list, (e.g., blamed, abandoned, anger).

1. _____

_____

2. _____

_____

3. _____

_____

Use each feeling in a sentence which best describes your feeling about your mother, (e.g., I feel blamed by my mother for all that's wrong in her life! If it wasn't for me, she would have divorced my Dad a long time ago.)

1. **I feel** _____

_____

_____

_____

_____

_____

_____

_____

_____

_____

_____

2. I feel _____

_____

_____

_____

_____

_____

_____

_____

3. I feel _____

_____

_____

_____

_____

_____

_____

_____

Father

Identify three feelings you have for your father from the feeling list, (e.g., blamed, abandoned, anger).

1. _____

_____

2. _____

_____

3. _____

_____

Use each feeling in a sentence which best describes your feeling about your father, (e.g., I feel abandoned by my father because he left us when I was nine years old. He never came back.)

1. I feel _____

_____

_____
_____
_____
_____
_____
_____
_____

2. I feel _____
_____
_____
_____
_____
_____
_____

3. I feel _____
_____
_____
_____
_____
_____
_____
_____
_____

PART TWO
Real and Ideal

Using the feeling list, select three feelings that you have for your real mother and father and three feelings that would like to have for your mother and father.

Real Feelings for Mother	Ideal Feelings for Mother
_____	_____
_____	_____
_____	_____

Real Feelings
for Father

_____

_____

_____

Ideal Feelings
for Father

_____

_____

_____

PART THREE
Painful, Sad and Frightening Experiences

Mother

Describe the most painful or hurtful experience you had with your mother.

(e.g., The most painful or hurtful experience I had with my mother was the time she called me a whore when I was 13 years old. I had tried so hard to be good and I _was_ good.

_____

_____

_____

_____

_____

Describe the saddest experience you had with your mother.

(e.g., The saddest experience I had with my stepmother was the time she left my father and cried for a long time, even though he had been so mean and hurtful towards her. I was 9 years old.)

_____

_____

_____

_____

_____

_____

_____

Describe the most frightening experience you had with your mother.

(e.g., The most frightening experience I had with my mother was the time she went out of control and beat my brother with a stick and then beat me.)

_____

_____

_____

_____

_____

_____

_____

_____

Father

Describe the most painful or hurtful experience you had with your father.

(e.g., The most painful or hurtful experience I had with my father was the time he was drunk and cried about his screwed up life. I held him in my arms like he was a baby. I was only 7 years old.)

_____

_____

_____

_____

_____

_____

Describe the saddest experience you had with your father.

(e.g., The saddest experience I had with my stepfather was my tenth birthday when I told him that I hated him and wished he were dead, and he cried.)

_____

_____

_____

_____

_____

_____

Describe the most frightening experience you had with your father.

(e.g., The most frightening experience I had with my father was the time he drove the car at 65 mph on a winding road and we all screamed for him to stop.)

_____

_____

_____

_____

PART FOUR
Conflictual Feelings

Mother

What two feelings do you have for your mother that seem opposite, yet true? (e.g., abandonment and nurturance.)

Explain: (e.g., abandonment and nurturance—I felt emotionally abandoned by my mother as she was often preoccupied with my father and then my stepfather. She spent most of her time getting things under control: my father and stepfather; the children; the drinking. However, she was always nurturing in a practical way. She made sure we had clothes, food, and a nice home. Although I felt hurt by her emotional absence, I was grateful that she took care of us since my father and stepfather didn't at all.)

Father

What two feelings do you have for your father that seem opposite, yet true? (e.g., pity and admiration.)

Explain: (e.g., pity and admiration—I feel pity for him because he drowned his many natural gifts in booze. He also drowned our relationship. As far as a father-son relationship, we had little time or closeness together. He was always distracted, even when we were together. Drinking, the pursuit of the next drink, and his career were his only concerns. I feel a lot of pity for him and all that he lost due to alcohol. Oddly enough, I also admired him for his skills and achievements. He was very well known and well liked (at least before his drinking got real bad). Sometimes when I'd look up at him, I felt proud. When I remember how much he achieved, I sometimes question whether his drinking problem was all that bad. Then I realize that I'm just heading for denial . . . again.)

NOTES

CHAPTER THIRTEEN

INSTRUCTIONS FOR LETTERWRITING TO PARENTS

Step One

Plan in advance the days you will write your letters. Choose one day for mother and another for father. Allow yourself at least 2 hours or more to write each letter. These letters are not to be sent to either parent; therefore, you are free to be as honest as you can be.

Step Two

At the top of the page, identify each parent by the name you call them, e.g., Dear Mommy, Dear Mother, Dear Dad, Dear Father.

Step Three

Review each worksheet to re-stimulate your feelings about each parent.

Step Four

Write your real feelings about each parent's role in your life and the effects of their behavior and attitudes on your ability to love yourself and others. Be specific about your hurts and resentments. Your feelings may seem to contradict each other. Trust that it is okay to have conflicting feelings about your parents.

Step Five

After you have completely exhausted your feelings about each parent, describe to each parent the kind of relationship you want to have or wish you could have had with them.

FORGIVENESS & COMPASSION COME WITH RECOVERY; THERE IS NO NEED TO FORCE THESE FEELINGS. LET THE FURY RIDE . . . THIS TOO SHALL PASS.

Example Letter to Mother

Dear Mom,

I feel so much anger towards you. I know that Dad was the drunk—you were the good one. It just doesn't seem right that I hate you so much, but I do. I hate you because all you thought about (while I was growing up) was Dad's drinking and your own misery. There wasn't anything left for me. I learned not to ask for or expect any attention after awhile. You had so little to give.

How could you keep yourself and me in such a miserable situation! Always waiting for him to straighten out; to grow up. He never did and neither did I! I still don't know how to manage my life. I feel so frightened and lonely even when everything in my life appears to be fine. I can't even figure out what normal is—I always seem to need someone else to tell me I'm okay.

It's not that you hit me or said mean things to me—you just didn't do anything at all. He was gone because of drinking. **WHAT WAS YOUR EXCUSE?** Where were you Mom? Where were you when I needed someone to talk to or when I needed some help? Probably going from bar to bar trying to track Dad down or over at your mother's house complaining about Dad and your rotten life.

Well, if it was so rotten, why didn't you do something about it? Why didn't you change it? Instead you acted like a poor, powerless victim. What a model for a child! No wonder I have trouble accepting responsibility for my life and my happiness. No wonder I don't take action to make things better. I grew up with someone who never did—NEVER! Goddammit, that makes me mad.

And furthermore, you expected me to take care of you. And what's saddest is that I tried—I still do. Just getting mad at you, even though (or especially because) you're dead, is so hard for me. I think of how you would dissolve into tears—of how hurt you'd be and I get sucked in all over again. Poor Mom! She had it so hard.

Well, Mom, no more! You made your choices and you were miserable, but it was not my fault. And it was not my job to make you happy. I used to cry myself to sleep thinking of how unhappy you were and feeling terrible because I couldn't think of some way to make you happy. Make you happy . . . of course I couldn't do that. I was a child and you were quite unhappy long before I ever came along.

Maybe if I hadn't gotten the idea that it was my duty to make you happy, I could have empathized with you more. Maybe I could have listened to your feelings without feeling suffocated with guilt and responsibility. I would have liked to have tried, Mom.

It just doesn't seem like I ever got the chance to really see you. There was so much I didn't get from you that I never saw you for who you were—an unhappy, confused person who really didn't know how to make things better. Part of me knows that you did try, Mom, and that you did want things better for yourself and for me. And part of me knows that you did love me—I do know that and I am grateful that I know it. I just wish we could have shared it more. And, Mom, I love you too.

Your daughter,

Linda   (Age 45)

Example Letter to Father

Dear Dad,

You are a great disappointment in my life. You had and still have the talent and intelligence to do anything that you want, but you took the easy way every time. Booze, cigarettes, a lousy marriage, a menial job—where along the line did you give up?

I am ashamed of your drunkeness; it's no wonder we never did anything together. Relationships take effort. The only effort you've ever exerted was to withdraw, tip the wine jug and wallow in your alienation and self-pity.

I am angry that I have to try so hard to not be the father you were. I have to fight to improve my marital relationship instead of withdrawing from it as you *did. I hate the stiffness and antisocial behavior that I seem to have inherited from you and your father. I WANT TO FEEL! I WANT TO BE ABLE TO CRY! I WANT TO HUG MY SON, KISS HIM AND SAY, "I LOVE YOU"! That's something you never did. God help me, I don't want to be like you in that way.*

I am angry that you didn't have the guts to send my stepmother away long ago! Where was your self-respect. You couldn't see the torture I went through to live with you. All you ever said was that she was jealous of me; BUT YOU NEVER STOOD UP FOR ME! Where's your backbone? It made me strong, but what do you expect of a child?

Why couldn't we talk? Why did we always argue? To this day, I fight myself not to get into arguments over unimportant things. Arguing and fighting was a daily routine. I must be making progress because I'm starting to feel that gut level pain again.

I shudder to think of all the emotion you keep inside. You don't fool me! Inside you are a sensitive and feeling person—do you think those feelings go away? They are poisoning you.

I've always had so much admiration for your patience, intelligence and kindness. It's amazing that there is anything left, but there is.

Dad, I just wish we could be together, have some good talks, with you sober. I wish we could re-establish a decent relationship. I don't want you to die with our relationship as it is. I would be so happy if you could stop drinking.

I love you, Dad!

Your son,

Bill   (Age 34)

CHAPTER FOURTEEN

OUR PERSONAL BILL OF RIGHTS

I Have a Right to Safety

As a child in an alcoholic home, you may have experienced physical or verbal abuse or physical or emotional neglect. You had no way of escaping your unsafe environment. The only way out may have been to deny your feelings and memories so that you could survive on a day-to-day basis.

Today, you may still find that you deny yourself a safe and supportive environment. Even though you are now in charge of your life, you may find that you seek out that which is familiar—unsafe or abandoning relationships and situations.

For some of you, your life may appear to be "under control." However, deep inside you continue to feel unsafe or abandoned. So much of your time may be spent attempting to appear "normal," while feeling confused and frightened inside. You may cling to people and situations that make you look good, even when it feels bad.

In recovery, we create quiet, alone time for ourselves. In this alone time, we find safety from within. We also create a home, work and play environment that does not violate our needs or rights. We learn to detach from or leave unsafe people, places or things in the name of self-love. We learn assessment skills regarding safety through conscious self observation and self-acceptance based on where we are in our recovery. TODAY, WE HAVE CHOICES.

I Have a Right to Have and Express Feelings

As a child in an alcoholic home, you may have experienced humiliation or condemnation for having feelings and for expressing them. There wasn't enough room for you to have feelings or needs. With little space or support, you may have learned to stuff, deny or numb out your feelings. You may also have learned to deny your own needs to avoid disappointment or hurt.

Today, you may still find that you deny your feelings and needs. It may feel overwhelming to acknowledge them. It is very familiar to deny, reject or minimize your feelings or needs for something or someone else. Your denial may even bolster your illusion of control. It may be too frightening to try something new. You may fear rejection and never try. Although we tend to seek the easy way out, there is hope.

In recovery, we create a support system of people who can understand and respect our feelings and needs. We no longer knock on the heart's door of someone who is not emotionally present or available. We attract and accept people who are loving. We relearn the language of feelings and take responsibility for our own feelings and behavior towards others. TODAY, WE HAVE CHOICES.

I Have a Right to Physical and Emotional Boundaries

As a child in an alcoholic home, you may have experienced an intrusive or abandoning parent. Your body, mind and spirit may have been intruded upon by your parent. Perhaps when you did say NO, or when you rebelled against unfair or abusive treatment, you were not heard or regarded as worthy of being treated with respect. Your rights to emotional and physical privacy may have been disregarded. You may have learned early on as a child that your feelings don't count. You may have learned to say YES to whatever demands were put upon you.

Today, you may still find that you allow other people to invade your privacy. You may not know how to set boundaries or simply how to say NO. It may frighten you to "rock the boat." It may even seem simpler and more satisfying to say YES and give in when you'd rather say NO.

In recovery, we learn to set limits with people, places and things in our life. In this way, we learn to respect our own privacy by standing up for ourselves and our needs, and we learn to respect the privacy and boundaries of others. We learn to say NO in a safe and serious way, so that we are heard and respected. We learn basic assertion skills to help us say NO in a loving but firm way. TODAY, WE HAVE CHOICES.

I Have a Right to Grieve

As a child in an alcoholic home, you may have learned to avoid feeling the pain which came with the loss of your childhood. You may have learned not to show your feelings or to cry. Perhaps when you did cry there was no one there to hold or comfort you. Perhaps your family lived from crisis to crisis, which did not allow time for grieving. You may have reacted to crisis after crisis by adopting the compulsive behaviors of the adults in your life to get relief from the pain. This was not a choice you made; it was survival.

Today, you may still find that you can't cry much or maybe at all. Perhaps when you do let the sadness surface, it feels so overwhelming that you become afraid that if you cry, you will never stop. An avalanche of grief seems to be waiting to snow you under. You may tell yourself there isn't anything to be sad about today. You made it. You got out of your family just in the nick of time. Yet, you find strange compulsions taking over your life. What appears to give you relief actually doesn't work. Overworking, overeating, over-reacting and overdoing—these are distractions to keep you from feeling anxiety or depression.

In recovery, we step out of the compulsive activities that we adopted to numb out the pain. We allow the grief to surface. As we walk through our grief, we find that we are not alone. We learn to turn to a power greater than ourselves who can help us heal our gaping wounds. We also walk with millions of other Children of Alcoholics on the path of recovery. TODAY, WE HAVE CHOICES.

I Have a Right to Talk

As a child in an alcoholic home, you may have experienced rejection and harrassment for acknowledging or talking about the real problem in your family—alcoholism and co-dependency. You may have been told that you were the problem that caused the alcoholic to drink and the co-dependent to cry or yell. You may also have been convinced that the things that were said and done during the "troubled times" didn't really happen. You may have learned to deny your reality, rationalize your dysfunctional behaviors and intellectualize your feelings.

Today, you may still find that you do not acknowledge or talk about your real problems. In fact, few people, if any, really know you. It's easier that way! For some of you, it may be hard for you to identify your feelings or your problems. You may experience free floating misery or anxiety. You may feel so cut off from your true self that reality may feel like a distant and unreachable experience. There is really nothing to share or acknowledge about you or your feelings. You may believe it's what you *do* that counts, not who you are.

In recovery, we share our feelings and memories of growing up in an alcoholic family with other people. We learn to break the family rule—DON'T TALK—by seeking others just like ourselves who will understand and support our recovery. We break the silence and isolation. We learn basic communication skills by joining groups and participating as best as we can. We build upon our communication skills one day at a time. TODAY, WE HAVE CHOICES.

CHAPTER FIFTEEN

READING AND RESOURCES

Reading Materials

IT WILL NEVER HAPPEN TO ME, by Claudia Black
(1982, M.A.C. Printing and Publications)

In-depth description of the roles assumed by children in alcoholic families and how those roles affect them as adults. Outstanding resource of information and support for Adult Children of Alcoholics.

REPEAT AFTER ME, by Claudia Black
(1985, M.A.C. Printing and Publications)

Excellent workbook for Adult Children of Alcoholics. Contains exercises for resolving childhood issues as well as changing the reader's present life.

ANOTHER CHANCE: HOPE AND HEALTH FOR THE ALCOHOLIC FAMILY, by Sharon Wegscheider
(1981, Science and Behavior Books)

Compassionate and detailed description of each member of the alcoholic family: their role; their issues; and their treatment. Includes chapters on the alcoholic and co-dependent as well as each childhood role.

CHOICEMAKERS, by Sharon Wegscheider-Cruse
(1985, Health Communications Inc.)

In-depth exploration of Co-Dependency in which the author shares her story and her path of recovery.

ADULT CHILDREN OF ALCOHOLICS, by Janet Woititz
(1983, Health Communications Inc.)

Very helpful description of the characteristics of Adult Children of Alcoholics.

STRUGGLE FOR INTIMACY, by Janet Woititz
(1985, Health Communications Inc.)

Explores the myths and issues of relationships and describes means for learning to build trust and intimacy in relationships.

HOPE FOR CHILDREN OF ALCOHOLICS, by Alateen
(1973, Al-Anon Family Group Headquarters, Inc., P.O. Box 182, Madison Square Station, New York, NY 10010)

A look at the Al-Anon/Alateen Program. Discusses the disease concept of alcoholism as it applies to the family. Contains personal stories by teens who have been helped by the program.

CO-ALCOHOLIC/PARA-ALCOHOLIC; WHO'S WHO AND WHAT'S THE DIFFERENCE, by Jael Greenleaf
(P.O. Box 30036, L.A., CA 90030)

A short paper which does a good job of outlining the characteristics of co-alcoholics and para-alcoholics.

AFFIRMATIONS: DAILY INSPIRATION FOR ADULT CHILDREN OF ALCOHOLICS, by Rokelle Lerner
(1985, Health Communications, Inc.)

It's exactly what the title suggests! Extremely supportive and encouraging daily readings.

WOMEN WHO LOVE TOO MUCH, by Robin Norwood
(1985, Tarcher/St. Martin's Press)

This book is for anyone who has ever "lost" themselves in or felt "addicted" to a relationship. Most Children of Alcoholics qualify, and Robin Norwood does an excellent job of describing the destructive patterns and offering suggestions for recovery.

THE DRAMA OF THE GIFTED CHILD, HOW NARCISSISTIC PARENTS FORM AND DEFORM THE EMOTIONAL LIVES OF THEIR TALENTED CHILDREN, by Alice Miller
(1981, Basic Books, Inc./Harper Colophon Books)

This book was originally published under the title *Prisoners of Childhood*. The characteristics of a narcissistic parent and an alcoholic or co-dependent parent are similar, and Alice Miller describes well the experience of growing up with either.

MAKING PEACE WITH YOUR PARENTS, by Harold Bloomfield
(1983, Random House)

A terrific book for anyone wanting to improve their present life by healing the old relationships with their parents. Contains exercises and practical suggestions for changing those relationships and one's life, as well as a specific chapter on "difficult parents."

Resources

The following is a list of the headquarters of several Anonymous Programs. All of these programs are based on the principles of Alcoholic Anonymous, and the local offices are listed in the telephone directory. If you are unable to find a local listing, contact the address below.

Alcoholics Anonymous (A.A.)
World Service Offiice
P.O. Box 459, Grand Central Station
New York, NY 10163
(212) 686-1100

Al-Anon Family Group Headquarters
World Service Office
P.O. Box 182, Madison Square Station
New York, NY 10159–0182
(212) 302-7240

Overeaters Anonymous
World Service Office
2190 190th Street
Torrance, CA 90504
(213) 320–7941

Narcotics Anonymous
World Service Office
16155 Wyandotte Street
Van Nuys, CA 91406
(818) 780-3951

CHAPTER SIXTEEN

A GUIDE FOR GROUP LEADERS

THE METHOD
Specialized Treatment and Support

The first question you might ask is, "Why do Adult Children of Alcoholics need specialized treatment and support?" While the counseling field has provided treatment and support for this group for years, that treatment has not focused on family alcoholism as the primary cause of problems. Today Adult Children of Alcoholics are joining groups which do focus on alcoholism and deal with the problems and issues that are a direct consequence of growing up in an alcoholic home. More than that, they are accepting an identity as Adult Children of Alcoholics that makes sense of their past and present feelings.

Groups for Adult Children of Alcoholics are a mixture of people from all walks of life. The stories, the sadness and the laughter allow even the unlikeliest of companions to join together as a group in recovery. Through the differences and similarities, Children of Alcoholics are able to break the silence, which in and of itself is healing.

Again, why do Adult Children of Alcoholics need specialized treatment and support? **BECAUSE IT WORKS.**

Recovery

Another question you might ask is, "What does recovery mean for Adult Children of Alcoholics?" One meaning of the word recovery is to get or obtain something lost. A most treasured possession that Children of Alcoholics lost is their childhood and the opportunity to develop to their fullest potential. For Adult Children of Alcoholics, recovery is a regression backwards for a more thorough and healthy progression forwards. For most Adult Children of Alcoholics reclaiming the negative as well as the positive memories of their childhood instills a sense of wholeness. Life for Children of Alcoholics did not begin at 18 years old. Reclaiming their childhood and relearning basic living skills are essential for their progression into full adulthood.

The Back Door Method

The Breaking The Silence Workbook uses three methods to restimulate memories and feelings. These methods are: questions directed to the Child-Within; quotes and examples by other Children of Alcoholics; and having the participants use Cat Family pictures to tell stories of family dynamics. The "back door method" reaches back in time to that tender child whose voice has been forgotten. Reading aloud from the workbook both liberates and strengthens the voice of the Child-Within and the resulting recognition of the loss of childhood allows the grief process to begin.

The Breaking the Silence Workbook was originally designed for "acting out" adolescents in residential treatment. These adolescents were unable to talk about their feelings, their families or themselves. Since they were already the "identified patient," it was diffiicult for them to see their current problems as stemming from the alcoholic family system. Their behaviors were so hostile and inappropriate it was easy for staff and other professionals to get hooked on wanting to fix or change their behaviors, rather than addressing their dysfunctional family system. Focusing on the real culprit in the family—Alcoholism and Co-Dependency—allowed these adolescents to experience relief. No longer were they to blame! Acknowledging their feelings, sharing their experiences and addressing their behaviors created an atmosphere of compassion and acceptance. Families were reunited in a healthy way—the "real" problems faced rather than denied.

I found that the participants in my workshops with Adult Children of Alcoholics experienced the compassion and acceptance in much the same way as the adolescents had. At first, I thought the adults would find the written exercises too simple and the Cat Family Pictures too silly! But, I forged ahead, trusting that the "back door method" would reach the "real" client or the hidden client: the Child-Within each Adult Child of an Alcoholic. The "back-door method" proved to be a gentle yet direct way of unveiling the effects of alcoholism on the child in the alcoholic family.

Safety Through Structure

Due to the structure of the Breaking the Silence Workshop, Adult Children of Alcoholics can share their experiences and their grief without pressure to "hurry up and get better" in the present. The workbook is designed to help Children of Alcoholics share their memories and feelings in a safe and structured way. Children of Alcoholics tend to write about their past more honestly than they speak about it. The written exercises and Cat Family pictures provide a way to relieve the participant of the impulse to deny, minimize or exaggerate their childhood experiences.

Some Children of Alcoholics suffer from memory loss. Listening to others share from their workbook stimulates memories that may have been forgotten or denied. It is wonderful to watch heads nodding in unison when a participant is sharing experiences to which most or all of them can relate. The similiarities far outweigh the differences. The acknowledgement of each other's loss and compassion for each other's pain allows for an even deeper experience of self acceptance and love.

For the most part, sharing out loud memories and feelings of growing up in an alcoholic home provides the necessary stimulation for insight. In fact, participants can more readily own and accept their insights about themselves when it comes from their own writings and in their own words. Individualized feedback by group leaders regarding a participant's past experiences and current behaviors is unnecessary.

One of the most positive results of the structure of Breaking the Silence Workshop is the participation of each person regardless of their past ability or strategy in group therapy. Children of Alcoholics tend to lean on survival roles to avoid being a participant in life and in therapy. The use of overtalk, no-talk and distracting methods to avoid feelings can be reduced by following the structure and the guidelines for leading workshops. Sharing one at a time by reading from the workbook allows each person to be a participant.

The 12 session workshop for most Adult Children of Alcoholics is a short enough period to commit to and a long enough one to inspire hope. By no means is this workshop designed to be **"THE CURE"** or a substitute for long term recovery work. The Breaking the Silence Workshop is a method of opening the door called **GRIEF**. Each participant has a choice as to whether to walk through the door or not. Group leaders act as guides.

THE LOGISTICS
Recruitment of Participants

Most Alcohol and Drug Abuse Centers have a referral list for counselors who specialize in alcoholism or drug addiction and its effects on the family. Contacting your local center for referrals and professional resources is an excellent way to recruit participants for a Breaking the Silence Workshop.

Another means of recruitment is free introductory lectures for Adult Children of Alcoholics on the effects of alcoholism on the child in the alcoholic home. There are many books available about Children of Alcoholics on the resource list in this workbook that will aid you in developing a lecture. Your visibility as a group leader for Adult Children of Alcoholic groups will enable potential participants to feel more comfortable and safe in their decision to work on recovery with you. Getting the word out on your free lecture for Adult Children of Alcoholics may include posting flyers, contacting other professionals and organizations and public service announcements on radio or in newspapers.

Screening

Screening participants is a responsible way of expressing care and concern for Adult Children of Alcoholics. It will also reduce the drop-out rate, which is important since the loss of group members often affects the morale of the group.

Some of the problems that should be assessed through a screening process are current drinking habits, emotional stability and current life situations (e.g. divorce, death of family member) that may interfere with participation. The initial stages of treatment are so stimulating for most people that it is essential that participants have basic coping skills. Individual counseling with a client for two to three months, or longer, is an effective way of screening, developing rapport and assessing suitability for a Breaking the Silence Workshop.

Screening is especially important for the early recovering alcoholic/addict. I recommend that recovering alcoholics/addicts have a solid foundation of recovery prior to participating in a Breaking the Silence Workshop. For most alcoholics/addicts, this takes one or more years of active recovery in Alcoholics Anonymous or Narcotics Anonymous. Partipation in AA or NA helps in the development of internal support skills. These skills are necessary for coping with the resurgence of feelings and memories that occurs in the Breaking the Silence Workshop. Many early recovering alcoholics/addicts find Adult Children of Alcoholics recovery work overstimulating and overwhelming. However, later in recovery, it is essential that alcoholics/addicts who are also Children of Alcoholics pursue an active recovery program that deals with growing up in an alcoholic home.

A long term therapy group may be organized after the completion of the workshop. The process of re-committment for long term group therapy for Adult Children of Alcoholics is extremely important and must be addressed in a serious and systematic way. Another screening is necessary for participation in long term therapy groups so that the client and therapist can address the appropriateness for long term therapy work at the time for each individual and their needs.

Additional Support

Additional support from the group leader may be necessary for some participants in Breaking the Silence Workshop. The stress of the grief process (coming out of denial, facing fears and feeling angry and sad) may create overwhelming fear and anxiety in the present. Individual counseling, outside of the group, is the best way to provide the additional support needed. In this way, the participant will not use the group time for problem solving. Therefore, the maximum benefit is experienced by all. There is no need to disrupt the grief process of the group for the needs of one person—that is TOO FAMILIAR for Children of Alcoholics. The group leader must be committed to the process and the needs of ALL the participants.

Group Size

Eight participants is the ideal number for a Breaking the Silence Workshop.

Environment

Privacy is of the upmost importance in selecting a suitable room. The environment should be free of ringing telephones and intrusions by other staff members. A room with moveable chairs and adequate space for breaking down into duos is best.

THE FORMAT

The format is basically the same each session. A specific issue is covered in the homework and then in the group meeting. The format's predictability reduces the participants' anxiety and resistance.

Each session is 1½–2 hours long. The group leader needs to stay aware of the meeting's goals and the time allotted to meet those goals. Following the format will greatly reduce distractions from the issues and help the group to meet the goals of each meeting. However, the group leader may need to eliminate some of the exercises so that the group begins and ends on time.

This workshop is designed to be a historical review. Hence, it is important that the "here and now" process work be resisted and that the group remain focused on the workbook material.

Warm-Up

During the warm-up, the group leader makes any necessary announcements and informs the group of any reported absences. Because it is not unusual for group members to feel slighted by or blamed for another's absence, it is important to inform the group of absences. It is also important that group members know that they are required to report any absences, planned or unplanned.

The warm-up of each session also focuses on identifying feelings about the week's homework, in terms of the participants' resistance or ease in doing it. This process helps the members to become present for this meeting and to get connected with each other in a relaxed way.

Exercises

Each chapter includes several questions that are to be filled out as homework each week. Having completed the homework, the participants will be emotionally prepared to share their writings in a safe way. The exercises provide the safety and structure for self disclosure by each participant.

Sharing Cat Family Stories

Participants will relate to some of the Cat Family pictures but probably not to all of them. Likewise each participant will find some pictures more stimulating than others. For this reason I ask for volunteers to share their stories rather than having every participant share each week. Volunteering allows the participants to share stories that are most significant to them.

Allow ten to fifteen minutes for the Cat Family stories.

Wrap-Up

The wrap-up of the meeting is a time for the group leader to make any summary comments and refocus the group in the present. During this time, the participants may share their feelings about their emotional changes; they may also express a need for additional support. Listening to the concerns, fears or new awarenesses will often be enough. For those who express extraordinary need for support and help with their current problems, suggest individual counseling.

Wrap-up is also the time for assigning homework.

THE WORKSHOP
Session One
Introduction to
Breaking the Silence Workshop

Goals

● To become acquainted with each other.

● To express personal concerns or fears in discussing family issues and personal secrets.

● To explain how to use the workbook.

● To introduce the participants to the Child-Within Concept.

Procedure
Warm-Up

Begin the group by welcoming the participants to the Breaking the Silence Workshop.

Discuss the Guidelines of the Breaking the Silence Workshop. The discussion may include:

- the difference between a "here and now" long term therapy group and the Breaking the Silence Workshop.

- the homework as a method for recording and sharing in a structured and safe way.

- the use of experiential exercises that will assist in the restimulation of childhood memories (such as the Child-Within Meditation, anger work and reading aloud from the Workbook.

Exercise 1 - Participant Introduction

Ask the participants to write down three problems in their lives today that result from their being raised in an alcoholic home (e.g., free-floating anxiety, loneliness, fear of intimacy, fear of passing problems onto their children).

Ask participants to turn to the person next to them and introduce themselves and share their three problems.

Ask the participants to introduce themselves to the large group and repeat the information that they already shared in the duo with the large group.

Exercise 2 - Introduction to the Child-Within Concept

Distribute the *Breaking the Silence Workbook* and ask the group to turn to Chapter Two - How to Use This Workbook.

Instruct the participants to bring a photograph of themselves to the next meeting.

Discuss the Child-Within concept as described in Chapter Two.

Exercise 3 - Child-Within Meditation

Ask the participants to imagine an old photograph of themselves as a child. Proceed with the Child-Within Meditation Tape or read the following:

Close your eyes. Find a comfortable position and take a deep breath. Whenever you close your eyes, you will instantly relax, as you are relaxing now . . . letting go of all tension and resentment. PAUSE.

Take another deep breath and as you exhale feel yourself relax . . . follow along with my voice as best as you can. Allow the following thoughts to come into your awareness:

"I'm able to relax more and more in everything I do. I have every right to be here. I'm glad I'm here. I feel safe and comfortable with my right to be alive. I don't have to hurry because I'm right on time. PAUSE.

"I love myself with all my imperfections. I love myself with all my heart. I like being alone, and I like being with other people. I don't have to do tricks to get approval. PAUSE.

"Everyday in every way I am practicing self love. I am good enough to be loved by myself and others. I am no longer looking for the right person. I am the right person. PAUSE.

"I am free of fear and resentment. I am able to receive love from others. I no longer control others to feel love. I am love. I can trust my feelings. PAUSE.

"I am able to form intimate and loving relationships. I no longer seek abandonment. I seek love. I no longer seek emptiness. I seek fulfillment. I am on a path of self love." PAUSE.

Breathe deeply and continue to relax. Imagine for a moment, a picture or an image of yourself as a young child. PAUSE. Deep inside you is a beautiful and lovable child. Imagine your child. Imagine him or her in a garden . . . a lovely, quiet garden. PAUSE.

Enter the garden as the adult you are today. See the child. Feel your heart's door open . . . feel love for that little child. PAUSE.

Reach down and hold the child in your arms. Accept your child as needful for affection and love . . . Tell your child, "I accept you." PAUSE. Imagine your child asking for safety.

Tell your child, "I will protect you." PAUSE. Imagine your child asking for attention. Tell your child, "I love giving you attention." PAUSE. Imagine your child asking to be believed. Tell your child, "I believe you." PAUSE.

Spend a few moments with your child in a dialogue. PAUSE.

The more you love the Child-Within the more you grow in love. When you feel comfortable, open your eyes and return to the room.

Exercise 4 - Sharing

Ask the participants to share with the person next to them their feelings about the meditation. After the participants have shared in duos, ask them to share in the group.

Wrap-Up

Homework Assignment
1. Read Chapters One, Two and Three.
2. Fill out Chapter Four—Feelings.
3. Bring a photograph of self as a child.

Session Two
Feelings

Goals

●To welcome each participant's Child-Within into the group through sharing the photographs.

●To orient the group to the language of feelings.

●To share stories and restimulate feelings and memories.

Procedure
Warm-Up
Exercise 1 - Welcoming the Child-Within

Ask each participant to show their photograph to the group and briefly describe: why they selected that picture and their family structure. Each participant shares one at a time with the group. After each participant has spoken, the group leader welcomes the Child-Within by saying, "_____(name)_____, I'm glad you're here. Welcome!"

Exercise 2 - Expression of Feelings

Ask the participants to turn to Part One of Chapter Four, select three feelings from Mother's Expression of Feelings and their reasons for their rating, and share with the group. After each participant has shared, ask the participants to select three feelings from Father's Expression of Feelings and their reasons for their ratings, and share with the group.

Exercise 3 - Feelings Today

Ask the participants to share from Part Two with the person next to them, feelings that describe their expression of feelings today and how they are affected today by their parents' expression of feelings towards or around them as children.

Sharing Cat Family Stories
Wrap-Up

Homework Assignment: Fill out Chapter Five - Anger.

Session Three
Anger

Goals

●To identify learned expression of anger.

●To identify messages learned about expressing anger.

●To assess ability to set limits.

●To share stories and restimulate feelings and memories.

Procedure
Warm-Up
Exercise 1 - Expression of Anger

Ask the participants to share from Part One of Chapter Five, beginning with three ways Mother showed her anger. After each participant has shared, ask the participants to share Father's three ways.

Exercise 2 - Anger Today

Ask the participants to turn to the person next to them and share from Part Two, the three ways they show their anger today.

Exercise 3 - Anger History

Ask the participants to turn to Part Three and select one of the three anger histories (Childhood, Adolescence or Adulthood) to read aloud to the group one at a time.

Exercise 4 - Feelings About Anger History

Ask the participants to read Part Four to the person sitting next to them.

Sharing Cat Family Stories
Wrap-Up

Homework Assignment: Fill out Chapter Six - Fear.

Session Four
Fear

Goals
●To identify fears related to family rituals and routines.

●To identify behaviors that have developed as a result of fear.

●To assess how past and current fears block fulfillment today.

●To share stories and restimulate feelings and memories.

Procedure
Warm-Up
Exercise 1 - Fears Around Rituals and Routines

Ask the participants to select one area of fear from Part One of Chapter Six (e.g., mealtimes, bedtime, school, holidays, birthdays) to share with the group. Ask them to comment also on the frequency of the situation that was fearful for them as a child (e.g., often, rarely, never).

Exercise 2 - Fears Behaviors

Ask each participant to share from Part Two three things they did when they felt fearful as a child. Ask them to comment on whether these behaviors are ones they still do today.

Exercise 3 - Fears Today

Ask each participant to select from Part Three a fear they have today to read aloud to the group.

Sharing Cat Family Stories
Wrap-Up

Homework Assignment: Fill out Chapter Seven - Guilt.

Session Five
Guilt

Goals

●To identify guilt inducers that your parents used or continue to use to control or manipulate family members' decisions and behavior.

●To identify behavior developed in response to guilt inducers.

●To identify secret guilts from childhood, adolescence and adulthood.

●To initiate self-forgiveness.

●To share stories and restimulate feelings and memories.

Procedure
Warm-Up
Exercise 1 - Guilt Inducers

Ask each participant to share from Part One of Chapter Seven the three guilt inducers that Mother used or continues to use to control or manipulate family members. After each participant has shared, ask them to share three guilt inducers that Father used or continues to use to control or manipulate family members.

Exercise 2 - Secret Guilts

Ask participants to share their secret guilts from Part Two by turning to the person next to them and reading them aloud. NOTE: Encourage them to avoid giving explanations.

Exercise 3 - Forgiveness

Ask each participant to read aloud Part Three to the group including the statement "I forgive myself today." NOTE: Allow time for a brief discussion on feelings about self-forgiveness.

Sharing Cat Family Stories
Wrap-Up

Homework Assignment: Fill out Chapter Eight - Crying.

Session Six
Crying

Goals

●To identify ways sadness, especially crying as an expression of sadness or hurt, was denied or expressed by parents.

●To assess resistance to crying.

●To identify messages, behavior and ability to cry.

●To share stories and restimulate feelings and memories.

Procedure
Warm-Up

Exercise 1 - Expression of Sadness or Hurt

Ask participants to turn to Part One of Chapter Eight and share situations in which Mother openly expressed sadness or hurt through crying. After each participant has shared, ask them to share situations in which Father openly expressed sadness or hurt through crying.

Exercise 2 - Crying Today

Ask participants to share from Part Two three ways they resist crying today.

Exercise 3 - Crying History

Ask participants to select from Part Three one of their crying histories (Childhood, Adolescence or Adulthood) and read aloud to the group.

Sharing Cat Family Stories
Wrap-Up

Homework Assignment: Fill out Chapter Nine - Grief.

Session Seven
Grief

Goals

●To identify family members or friends that have been lost to death, alcoholism, mental illness, abandonment, or separation.

●To distinguish real feelings from idealized feelings about family members or friends.

●To identify stages of grief for family members or friends.

●To share stories and restimulate feelings and memories.

Procedure
Warm-Up

Exercise 1 - The Losses

Ask participants to share from Part One of Chapter Nine the name of the family member or friend that they selected and a brief description of the means of loss.

Exercise 2 - Real and Ideal Feelings

Ask participants to share from Part Two their real feelings and their ideal feelings towards family members or friends that they selected.

Ask them to comment on the difference between real and ideal feelings if there is a difference.

Exercise 3 - Stages of Grief

Ask participants to select from Part Three one of the Stages of Grief about a family member or friend, preferably the one they described in detail in Part Four, and share with the group.

Ask the participants to read their comments from Part Four aloud to the group.

Sharing Cat Family Stories
Wrap-Up

Homework Assignment: Fill out Chapter Ten - Sex Roles.

Session Eight
Sex Roles

Goals

●To identify feelings that men generally feel, that women generally feel and that both feel.

●To identify how sex role expectations affected the expression of feelings.

• To describe messages and behaviors learned regarding sex role expectations.

• To share stories and restimulate feelings and memories.

Procedure
Warm-Up

Exercise 1 - Men/Women/Feelings

Ask participants to share from Part Two of Chapter Ten five feelings that men have access to or express and read aloud their explanation for each feeling. Ask participants to share from Part Two, five feelings that women have access to or express and read aloud their explanation for each feeling.

Exercise 2 - Owning the Feelings

Ask participants to re-read the list of the five feelings of their *same sex parent* and own the feelings. For example, "Women feel worried because they can't control their spouses behavior or drinking." — "I feel worried because I can't control my spouse's behavior or drinking."

Allow each participant to comment on how it feels to own the feelings that they read. Often participants will acknowledge that they have the same or similar feelings as the ones they described.

Exercise 3 - Sex Role Expectations

Ask each participant to read aloud Part Three on how they were affected by sex role expectations in their family.

Sharing Cat Family Stories
Wrap-Up

Homework Assignment: Fill out Chapter Eleven - Relationships.

Session Nine
Relationships

Goals
• To identify parents' relationship to their parents.

• To describe parents' marital relationship.

• To identify approval-seeking behavior.

• To identify ability to be intimate in relationships.

• To describe an ideal intimate relationship.

• To share stories and restimulate feelings and memories.

Procedure
Warm-Up

Exercise 1 - Generational View

Ask each participant to share from Part One of Chapter Eleven, their Mother's relationship with her parents. After each has shared, ask them to share their Father's relationship with his parents. NOTE: This exercise assists the participants in recognizing the generational effects of alcoholism. Sometimes active alcoholism skips generations; however, the behavior patterns and thinking often remain unchanged generation to generation.

Allow a brief time for discussion.

Exercise 2 - Parents' Marriage

Ask each participant to share from Part Two the kind of marriage they think their parents had.

Exercise 3 - Approval Seeking Behavior

Ask each participant to share from Part Three the approval or attention seeking behavior they developed in their childhood, and ask them to comment on whether these behaviors are ones they continue to use today.

Exercise 4 - Relationships Today

Ask participants to share from Part Four the kind of intimate relationships they often have today. Ask them to share their three feelings that describe how they feel in intimate relationships.

Exercise 5 - Ideal Relationship

Ask participants to share their ideal relationship with the person sitting next to them.

Sharing Cat Family Stories
Wrap-Up

Homework Assignment: Fill out Chapter Twelve - Parents.

Session Ten
Parents

Goals
●To identify feelings about parents.

●To identify painful, sad and frightening experiences with parents.

●To identify conflictual feelings about parents.

Procedure
Warm-Up

Exercise 1 - Feelings About Parents

Ask each participant to share from Part One of Chapter Twelve the three feelings about Mother by reading the sentences aloud that begin with "I feel . . . " After each participant has shared, ask them to share the three feelings about Father by reading the sentences aloud that begin with "I feel . . . "

Exercise 2 - Real vs. Ideal

Ask each participant to share from Part Two three feeling words that describe their real feelings about Mother and three feeling words that describe their ideal feelings about Mother.

After each participant has shared, ask them each to share three feeling words that describe their real feelings about Father and three feelings words that describe their ideal feelings about Father. NOTE: Ideal feelings are ones that they wish they felt towards their parents.

Exercise 3 - Experiences with Parents

Ask each participant to share from Part Three one of the three experiences (e.g., painful, saddest or frightening) that they had with their Mother and share with the group.

After each participant has shared, ask them to select one of the three experiences that they had with their Father and share with the group.

Exercise 4 - Conflictual Feelings

Ask each participant to share from Part Four the conflictual feelings about Mother and Father with the person sitting next to them.

Wrap-Up

Homework Assignment: Fill out Chapter Thireteen - Letterwriting to Parents.

Session Eleven
Letters to Parents

Goals
- To role-play family interactions.

- To share letters to parents.

- To restimulate feelings and memories.

Procedure
Warm-Up

Exercise 1 - The Role-Play

Ask for a volunteer to role-play how they feel about family members today. (Additional resource: *Another Chance; Hope & Health for the Alcoholic Family*, Sharon Wegscheider, p. 234, Exercise 6: Posing the Family Portrait, originated by Virginia Satir.)

The volunteer asks one person at a time to role-play significant family members (mother, father, siblings, grandparents) from their primary family.

The volunteer places each person in physical distance to them based on their relationship and feelings towards each family member (e.g., "My mother stands directly facing me. As a child she and I were very close. In many ways we were partners in raising the other children. My relationship with her was the most powerful influence on my life. My mother still depends on me and is unwilling to let me go. I love her more than anyone, yet I feel a lot of pressure from her to make her life better. I can't seem to move past her or her needs.")

After each family member is placed and briefly discussed by the volunteer, the group leader asks the volunteer to speak directly to each "family member" one at a time. Instruct the volunteer to share with each "family member" any new insights or feelings about this family member and especially how they feel their relationship was affected by the alcoholic

environment. The "family member" is instructed to *react* or *respond* to any information or feelings shared by the volunteer.

NOTE: This is role-play. It may not be completely accurate. It is another way of restimulating feelings and memories. However, often the selection of the "family members" will be based on the similarities to their primary family. Therefore, all of the participants often benefit and are affected by the role-play.

Allow time after the role-play for a brief discussion by the group on how they were affected by the role-play.

Exercise Two - Sharing the Letters to Parents

Ask each participant to read aloud their letters from Chapter Thirteen to the person next to them. After the participants have shared with one person ask for volunteers to read their letters to the group.

Wrap-Up

Session Twelve
Family and Friends

Goals

- To inspire hope in the participants and their family and friends.

- To introduce the Al-Anon Program and Therapeutic Recovery through a personal story shared by a guest speaker.

- To acknowledge the negative and positive effects of recovery for participants and for their family and friends.

- To discuss the Stages of Recovery and the necessity of ongoing self-reflection through Al-Anon and treatment.

Procedure
Warm-Up

Exercise 1 - The Welcome

Welcome the families and friends of the participants. Ask each to say their name and identify their relationship to the participant with whom they have come.

Exercise 2 - The Speaker

Invite a speaker to share the experience, strength and hope of their own recovery as an Adult Child of an Alcoholic. Select a speaker who has had two years of active recovery as an Adult Child of an Alcoholic in Al-Anon Adult Children and therapy.

NOTE: Ask the speaker to talk for at least twenty minutes. Allow time for questions and comments.

Exercise 3 - Sharing by Family and Friends

Ask family and friends to share their impressions or feelings in regards to how they were affected by relating to a participant of the Breaking the Silence Workshop.

NOTE: The responses of family and friends vary. However, there is always a response of some kind.

Exercise 4 - Today

Ask each participant to share their feelings about the Breaking the Silence Workshop and its effect on their life today.

Exercise 5 - Recovery

Share with the group the Stages of Recovery as discussed in Chapter One. Emphasize to the participants the necessity of ongoing recovery work (e.g., Al-Anon, therapy, support groups). Emphasize to family and friends the necessity of support and understanding for the participants ongoing recovery work.

Wrap-Up